CAKES and FROSTINGS
with Schmecks Appeal

EDNA STAEBLER

McGRAW-HILL RYERSON
Toronto   Montreal

McCLELLAND & STEWART
Toronto

Cakes and Frostings with Schmecks Appeal

© 1991 by Edna Staebler

First published in 1991 by

MCGRAW-HILL RYERSON LIMITED
330 Progress Avenue
Scarborough, Canada
M1P 2Z5

MCCLELLAND & STEWART LIMITED
481 University Avenue
Suite 900
Toronto, Canada
M5G 2E9

1 2 3 4 5 6 7 8 9 0   W   0 9 8 7 6 5 4 3 2 1

ISBN: 0-7710-8273-8

CANADIAN CATALOGUING IN PUBLICATION DATA
Staebler, Edna, date
  Cakes and frostings with schmecks appeal

(Schmecks appeal cookbook series)

ISBN 0-7710-8273-8

1. Cake. 2. Icings, Cake. 3. Cookery, Mennonite.

4. Cookery - Ontario - Waterloo (Regional municipality).
I. Title. II. Series: Staebler, Edna, date. The schmecks appeal cookbook series.

TX771.S58 1991   641.8'653   C90-095544-9

Printed and bound in Canada

CONTENTS

CAKE IS A MIRACLE THING

My first encounter with cake came when I was barely tall enough to reach the hanging corner of the tablecloth on our big square kitchen table. Mother had run across the street to borrow an egg from Mrs. Hessenhauer and I was left playing alone on the kitchen floor. With the bright-blue enamel mixing bowl on the edge of the table where Mother had been stirring up a cake. It didn't take me long to give the tablecloth a tug that brought the bowl down on my lap. Mother found me blissfully licking the creamy batter that slathered me from head to toes. I've liked licking cake batter ever since.

Whenever people told Mother she was a fabulous cook — and everyone who ate at our house said that — Mother would say with a show of modesty that she hadn't baked a cake till after she was married. We never knew whether that meant she was proud of not having been taught to cook by her grandmother, who brought her up to be a lady, or whether her pride was in having taught herself how to follow a recipe successfully.

Mother didn't teach us how to bake either. When she stirred up a cake, she gave us jobs that kept us out of her way in the kitchen. "Norma and Ruby, you can straighten up the living room; Edna, you can dust the front stairway," and I'd be banished to those shapely cherry-wood spindles — three on each step — up that long curving staircase from the hall to the high ceiling and along the balustrade on the second floor, the place in the house farthest from the good kitchen smells. Maybe that's why I still avoid dusting and enjoy baking.

There's something magical about putting together things that are inedible by themselves — like flour, baking powder, baking soda, cocoa, cinnamon, buttermilk, or whatever — and blending them to make something completely different and delectable like a *cake*. A layer cake, a square or a round one, a big oblong cake, a rich fruity loaf cake to be cut in thin slices, a cake to be served with coffee or tea, with fruit or ice cream, as a dessert by itself, slathered with icing or a glaze, a cake is a creative accomplishment that can be enjoyed from the batter to the last crumb.

People have said to me, "I never make cakes. They're too chancy." Of course they are. Part of the adventure and fun is the uncertainty. One day I'll make a cake that is moist, tender,

1

and delicious; next time it might be coarse and soggy, or high, dry, and tasteless as a sponge. I don't know why. Maybe I forgot something vital or baked it too long; maybe I didn't follow the recipe exactly; maybe the recipe was faulty; maybe I substituted an ingredient that didn't work; maybe all the ingredients weren't at room temperature when I started; maybe my oven temperature was wrong. Once I forgot to put in the flour and baking soda. If I were a food chemist, I'd probably have all the answers; all I know about baking I've found out by trial and error after error after error. But I keep on baking cakes, dry, soggy, or perfect.

A multitude of errors can be smothered by a sticky or fluffy icing. Sprinkled with toasted nuts, who cares what's underneath? If you reheat a cake and serve it with a custard or a fudge sauce, who's to know you hadn't intended it to be a pudding in the first place? Or a sherry-laden trifle? And like cake batter, icing is good licking, too.

SMALL CAKES

DATE OATMEAL CAKE
8" x 8"

This cake from *Food That Really Schmecks* was the Grand Prize Winner of the 10th Anniversary Competition of *Homemaker's Magazine*. People sent in the recipe they liked best of all those published in the magazine in ten years. This was the favourite. Surely 1,232,000 homemakers couldn't be wrong.

Pour **1 cup boiling water** over **2 cups rolled oats**, mix well, cool slightly, then blend in:

¾ cup butter or margarine
2 cups brown sugar
2 eggs
1½ cups finely chopped dates
1 cup coarsely chopped walnuts

Sift together:
½ cup flour
1 teaspoon baking soda
½ teaspoon salt
1 teaspoon cinnamon
1 teaspoon ground cloves

Pour the oatmeal mixture into the dry ingredients and mix well. Bake in a greased 8" x 8" pan at 350°F for 45 minutes, or until done. It is so moist and rich it hardly needs icing — but, if you insist, use one made with brown sugar.

BUTTERING A PAN

You don't have to bother buttering the cake pan for a cake that isn't going to be inverted and taken out whole. Serve it in the pan and cut it as you use it with a bread knife or spatula or pie server that lifts it out clean. (I have pretty padded wicker containers that fit all my Pyrex pans, and I put a whole cake on my table.)

CHOCOLATE CHIP DATE CAKE
8" x 8" or 9" x 9"

Whenever Norm serves this cake, I hear someone say, "Gee, this is good cake."

> 1½ cups boiling water
> 1 cup chopped dates
> 1 teaspoon baking soda
> ½ cup shortening
> 1 cup sugar
> 2 eggs, beaten
> 1 teaspoon vanilla
> 1½ cups flour
> ½ teaspoon salt
>
> *Topping:*
> ½ cup brown sugar
> 1 cup (6 oz.) chocolate chips
> ¼ cup walnuts

Pour boiling water over the dates, add baking soda and let cool. Cream the shortening and sugar, add the beaten eggs, vanilla, and the cooled dates. Sift the flour and salt together and stir into the date mixture. Beat well and pour into a greased 8" x 8" or 9" x 9" pan. To make topping, combine the brown sugar, chocolate chips, and walnuts; sprinkle them over the batter. Bake at 350°F for 45 to 50 minutes. The topping will be crisp, the cake light as a feather.

NORM'S YUMMY HONEY CAKE
8" x 8"

A tasty, tender little cake that you can stir up in no time — and eat as quickly.

1 cup boiling water
1 cup dates, finely chopped
¼ cup soft shortening
½ cup honey
½ cup brown sugar
1 teaspoon vanilla
1 egg
1½ cups flour
1 teaspoon baking powder
¾ teaspoon baking soda
½ teaspoon salt

Topping:
½ cup brown sugar
¼ cup butter
¼ cup fruit juice or milk
½ cup shredded coconut

Pour the boiling water over the dates and let them cool. Beat the shortening, honey, brown sugar, vanilla, and egg till well blended. Sift the dry ingredients into the creamed mixture, adding the cooled date mixture as you stir until well combined. Pour into an 8" x 8" pan and bake in a 350°F oven for about half an hour. Let the cake cool in the pan on a rack. Combine the topping ingredients and boil gently for 10 minutes. Pour and spread over the cooled cake and call your neighbours over.

MAPLE WALNUT CAKE
8" x 8"

On Kit McDermott's birthday, I stuck some sparklers into this neat little cake, Gerry Noonan played his harmonica; Vern and Carroll Allen and I sang "Happy Birthday" while the sparklers sparkled. Then we indulged ourselves with this truly flavourful cake.

> **⅓ cup butter or margarine**
> **2 eggs**
> **1 cup maple syrup**
> **1¼ cups flour**
> **2 teaspoons baking powder**
> **Pinch of salt**
> **1 cup walnuts, chopped not too fine**
> **Soft Maple Icing (page 76)**

Beat together butter, eggs, and syrup. Sift together flour, baking powder, and salt, and stir in gradually. Add walnuts. Pour in a square pan and bake at 350°F for about 25 minutes. Let cool before icing with a maple butter icing or — what I prefer — a thin glaze of maple butter that can be bought in a tin from my Mennonite friends at the Waterloo or Kitchener markets.

WEARY WILLIE CAKE
8" x 8"

Easy and fun to make. Light, tender, and delicious.

Into a measuring cup, break the **whites of 2 eggs**, add enough soft **butter** to half fill the cup, then fill the cup with **milk**. In a mixing bowl, measure **1½ cups flour sifted** with **2 teaspoons baking powder** and **1 cup sugar**; turn into the dry ingredients the contents of the measuring cup and beat all together for 5 minutes. Add a **teaspoon of any flavouring** you like, I prefer almond, and bake the cake for half an hour in a 350°F oven. The yolks of the eggs can be blended with powdered sugar to make an icing.

GUM DROP CAKE
8" x 8"

Bevvy bakes this for special events — like a wedding, or a gebutsdag (birthday).

½ cup butter
1 cup sugar
2 eggs, well beaten
1 cup milk
2½ cups flour
2 teaspoons baking powder
1 teaspoon nutmeg
1 teaspoon cinnamon
1 pound gum drops (no black ones), cut up
Basic Butter Icing (page 75)

Blend the butter and sugar, beat in the eggs; alternately add the milk and sifted dry ingredients, then the gum drops. Bake in a greased 8" x 8" pan at 350°F for 45 minutes. Ice with Basic Butter Icing and decorate with gum drops. It will be a hit.

BAD LUCK

If a cake doesn't rise as high as it ought to, you can cut it in small squares and serve it like brownies, or put a scoop of ice cream on top, or make it into pudding by heating it and serving it with a sauce.

Never despair: try another recipe, check the temperature of your oven. There's always another occasion, another day. Who knows: tomorrow you may make the cake of the century.

Once after one of my cake recipes was reprinted in the Hamilton *Spectator*, I received a letter from a woman who said she had tried it and it hadn't turned out the way I said it would; and she wanted to be reimbursed for the cost of the materials she had put into it: pumpkin, flour, milk, etc.

I wrote back to say that considering how many variables there are in cake-baking, if she had never in her life produced an unsuccessful cake, she was a very lucky lady.

B IS FOR BUTTERMILK

In all my own cookbooks, I've written a large B in the margin beside the cakes that are made with buttermilk; I think they are moister and more flavourful. Besides, they give me a good way to use up surplus buttermilk. It mustn't be kept too long, and I naturally wouldn't throw it away.

QUICKIE CRUMB CAKE
9" x 9"

This is probably the quickest cake I know how to make. It doesn't have to be iced and can be served warm. I mix it in my food processor while the oven is warming up.

½ cup shortening
2 cups brown sugar
2½ cups flour
1 egg
1 teaspoon almond flavouring or vanilla
1 teaspoon baking soda dissolved in
1 cup buttermilk

Blend shortening, sugar, and flour. Take out ½ cup of this mixture and reserve. Add remaining ingredients. Pour batter into a 9" x 9" pan and sprinkle reserved crumbs on top. Bake at 350°F for about 30 minutes.

RHUBARB CRUMB CAKE
(from Serena Shantz)
9" x 9"

Tender, with a crispy cinnamon crust on top. Kit and Vern and I demolished almost an entire cake with our afternoon tea.

1½ cups brown sugar
½ cup shortening
1 egg
1 cup sour cream
1 teaspoon vanilla or almond flavouring
2 cups flour
1 teaspoon baking soda
1 teaspoon baking powder
2 or 3 cups diced rhubarb

Topping:
¼ cup sugar
½ teaspoon cinnamon
½ cup chopped nuts

Cream sugar and shortening. Beat in the egg, then stir in the sour cream with the flavouring. Sift the flour, baking soda, and baking powder together into the creamed mixture and blend thoroughly. Stir in the rhubarb. Spread in a 9" x 9" or larger pan, sprinkle with topping mixture, and bake at 350°F for 35 to 40 minutes, or until a toothpick inserted in the centre comes out clean. Serve warm. If you use frozen rhubarb, bake about 15 minutes longer.

CARROT CRUMB CAKE
9" x 9"

People keep thanking me for the wonderful carrot cake recipe in *Food That Really Schmecks*; they say there couldn't be a better one. I agree. But this carrot cake with the crumb topping from a Croatian lady in Saskatchewan is moist, light, delicious, and easier to prepare, especially if you have a blender.

After picking dandelion blossoms in my lawn to make wine, Pamela and Gerry Noonan and I ate the whole slightly warm cake at a sitting. No regrets.

½ cup soft margarine
1 cup sugar
1 egg
1½ teaspoons vanilla
1 cup buttermilk
1 to 1½ cups raw sliced or grated carrots
2 cups pastry flour
2 teaspoons baking powder
½ teaspoon baking soda
¼ teaspoon nutmeg
1 teaspoon salt

Topping:
½ cup brown sugar
4 tablespoons flour
3 tablespoons melted butter

If you have a blender, put the margarine, sugar, egg, vanilla, buttermilk, and raw carrots cut in slices, into the blender and keep whirling till the carrots are finely chopped. Pour the mixture over the flour, baking powder, baking soda, nutmeg, and salt sifted together. Stir till blended, then pour into a 9" x 9" cake pan. Sprinkle with the crumbed topping mixture and bake at 350°F for 45 minutes.

If you don't have a blender, you'll have to grate the carrots first. Cream the margarine and sugar, beat in the egg and vanilla, stir in the carrots and alternately add the buttermilk and sifted dry ingredients.

CAPE BRETON'S KELTIC LODGE

With her little children playing around her, Molly sat on the cribbing of an old dock at Neil's Harbour. I sat beside her. We didn't talk much. We looked at the clouds in the darkening sky. Molly pulled her gum out of her mouth and folded it in again; sometimes she cracked it.

Little Philip called, "Molly, here comes Lizzie Deaver."

"Why so she do." Molly greeted her friend with pleasure. Lizzie, a stout young woman with a top front tooth missing, shy at first because of me, kept covering her mouth with her hand. But soon she talked about going places.

"I'd like to go to England," she said.

"Would you?" Molly was surprised. "It's awful far."

"I know, but I'd like to see where they have the Queen."

"Yes, 'twould be good to see that." Molly nodded.

"I might go down to Sidney this fall," Lizzie said. "Does you good to git away."

"Yes, it doos," Molly agreed. "Some toime Oi'd loike to leave keeds behind and go away for a whole week."

"Where to?" I asked.

Molly's eyes were full of dreams. "Oi'd loike to go to Ingonish and stay at the Keltic Lodge where the Goverman General was to."

Lizzie gasped. "Oh, Molly, not with all them swells?"

"Whoi not?" Molly pulled out her gum. "They's only people. Pisses same as we."

"Yes, but they pays twenty dollars a day just for what they eats," Lizzie said.

"Moi Gohd, ye'd have to eat a lot to git twenty dollars worth into ye, wouldn't you now? What could they feed 'em would be worth twenty dollars?"

"Ain't got nothin' there we ain't got here, has they?"

Molly said, "Holy jumpin' Cheesus, Oi'd loike to go and foind out."

HURRY-UP CHOCOLATE CAKE
9" x 9"

You probably have this recipe but I want to make sure everyone else has it, too. It's always so moist, coarse, and chocolate that I often wonder why I ever try any other. Your little helpers will love making it.

> 1½ cups flour
> 1 cup sugar
> 3 rounded tablespoons cocoa
> 1 teaspoon baking powder
> 1 teaspoon baking soda
> ½ teaspoon salt
> 1 teaspoon vanilla
> 1 teaspoon vinegar
> ½ cup margarine or butter, melted
> 1 cup lukewarm buttermilk
> Mocha Icing (page 82)

Sift all the dry ingredients into a 9" x 9" cake pan. Stir them well to blend. Bump the pan up and down on your counter to level off. Make 3 hollows in the mixture with a spoon. Put the vanilla in one hole, the vinegar in another, and the melted margarine or butter in the third. Over all this, pour the lukewarm buttermilk. Stir and blend until batter is smooth with no flour showing. Thump it on the counter again. Bake in a 350°F oven for about half an hour. Leave in the pan to cool; ice with Mocha Icing and try to stop tasting before you've gone too far.

THE BEST COCOA CAKE
8" x 8"

With a smooth, moist texture, this really is a dandy. I've made it many times.

> ½ cup shortening
> 2 cups brown sugar
> 2 eggs, well beaten
> ½ cup cocoa
> ½ cup boiling water

½ cup buttermilk
1½ cups flour
1 teaspoon baking soda
½ teaspoon salt
1 teaspoon vanilla
Chocolate Butter Icing (page 75)

Cream the shortening, add the sugar and keep creaming. Add the well-beaten eggs and beat the mixture thoroughly. Dissolve the cocoa in boiling water and add the buttermilk. Combine with the first mixture. Sift together the flour, baking soda, and salt, add to the other mixture and beat again — with the vanilla. Butter a square cake pan, flour it, pour in the batter and bake in a 350°F oven for about 45 minutes. Cool and frost with Chocolate Butter Icing.

BEULAH'S DATE AND COCONUT CAKE
8" x 8"

Mother had great faith in Beulah's recipes. They usually turned out pretty well.

1 cup butter
1 cup brown sugar
2 eggs, slightly beaten
½ cup milk
1 cup sour cream
1½ cups flour
1 teaspoon baking soda
2½ cups dates, cut up
1 cup coconut
1 cup walnuts, chopped coarsely
Toasted Coconut Frosting (page 77)

Blend the butter and sugar, beat in eggs; alternately add the milk, cream, and sifted dry ingredients with the dates, coconut, and walnuts. Turn into a greased 8" x 8" pan and bake in a 350°F oven till cake tests done. Cover with Toasted Coconut Frosting.

CHOCOLATE BEET CAKE
9" x 9"

Sheila, who sells the delicious tarts at the Waterloo Market, raves about this moist and great-tasting cake. She gave me the recipe and I haven't yet had a chance to try it. I hope you will.

Combine:

> **1½ cups sugar**
> **2 large eggs**

Add:

> **1 cup oil**
> **2 cups beets, cooked and puréed (or use drained tinned beets)**

Stir in:

> **6 tablespoons cocoa**
> **1¾ cups flour**
> **1½ teaspoons baking soda**
> **¼ teaspoon salt**
> **1 teaspoon vanilla**

Beat 2 minutes at medium speed — or do it by hand. Pour into 9" x 9" pan and bake at 350°F for 45 to 50 minutes. Cool before icing.

> *Icing:*
> **2 tablespoons shortening**
> **1 tablespoon butter**
> **4 tablespoons cocoa**

Cream together then add:

> **2 cups icing sugar**
> **⅓ cup hot water**
> **¼ teaspoon peppermint extract (optional)**
> **⅛ teaspoon salt**

Beat until smooth.

RUM AND DATE CAKE
8" x 8"

Mother had to wangle this precious recipe from Mrs. Emil Schultz.

2½ cups dates (more is better, Mother says)
1 cup walnuts
1 teaspoon baking soda
1 cup boiling water
½ cup butter
1 cup brown sugar
2 eggs
1 cup flour
½ teaspoon salt
1 teaspoon vanilla
4 tablespoons rum
1 teaspoon water

Icing:
½ cup soft butter
1½ cups icing sugar
1 tablespoon rum

Chop dates and nuts, add baking soda to boiling water and pour over dates and nuts; let stand while preparing batter.

Cream butter and gradually add the sugar; beat eggs thoroughly and add to butter and sugar. Pour date mixture into this and mix well. Sift together flour and salt; add to mixture, adding vanilla last. Pour into greased 8" x 8" pan and bake at 350°F for one hour. Remove cake from oven and pour over it the rum mixed with a little water. Allow to cool before icing with blended icing ingredients. This cake keeps well and is moist and rummy and rich.

COUSIN LUCY'S SPICE CAKE
8" x 8"

My father's white-haired Cousin Lucy was considered one of the finest cooks in Grand Rapids, Michigan. We thought so anyway.

    Butter the size of an egg
    1 cup sugar
    1 egg, slightly beaten
    3 tablespoons molasses
    1½ cups flour
    1 teaspoon cinnamon
    ½ teaspoon baking powder
    ½ teaspoon baking soda
    Pinch of allspice
    1 cup buttermilk
    ¼ teaspoon vanilla
    Penuche Icing (page 84)

Cream the butter, blend in sugar, egg, and molasses. Sift the dry ingredients and add them to the egg mixture alternately with the milk and vanilla. Bake in a greased, square cake pan in a 350°F oven for about 45 minutes. Give it a Penuche Icing — it deserves it.

RAISIN SPICE CAKE
9" x 9"

An unpretentious little cake that tastes good and stays moist.

    ½ cup shortening
    1 cup sugar
    1 egg, well beaten
    1 cup buttermilk
    1 teaspoon vanilla
    1½ cups raisins
    2½ cups flour
    ½ teaspoon baking soda
    1 teaspoon salt

½ teaspoon cinnamon
½ teaspoon cloves
¾ cup chopped nuts

Topping:
¼ cup chopped nuts
¼ cup sugar

Cream the shortening and sugar, add the beaten egg, the buttermilk, vanilla, and raisins. Sift the flour, baking soda, salt, and
spices together, stir into the egg mixture. Blend well, but don't
overdo it. Stir in the ¾ cup nuts. Pour the batter into a 9" x 9"
cake pan, sprinkle the ¼ cup chopped nuts on top, then the ¼
cup sugar, and bake in a 350°F oven for about 40 to 50 minutes.
If you serve this with a scoop of maple-walnut ice cream, be
prepared to serve seconds and hand out the recipe.

MOTHER'S MAGIC SPICE CAKE
8" x 8"

Mother was mortified when the hostess at a party for pre-
schoolers told her I had refused a piece of birthday cake "because I only like my mother's spice cake when it goes down in
the middle like taffy."

½ cup butter
2 cups brown sugar
2 eggs
1½ cups flour
1 teaspoon baking soda
1 teaspoon cloves
1 teaspoon cinnamon
½ teaspoon nutmeg
¾ cup buttermilk

Blend the butter and sugar, add the eggs and beat them in; sift
the flour with the baking soda and spices and add them alternately with the buttermilk. Pour the batter into a greased
8" x 8" cake pan and bake in a 350°F oven for about 40 minutes.
If you're lucky, it will fall flat and you won't have to ice it.

SMALL AND EASY APPLE CAKE
8" x 8"

This is a good way to use up those shrivelling, winter-stored apples. The cake is very moist and would keep well if it weren't so irresistible.

>1 egg
>1 cup sugar
>¼ cup vegetable oil
>2 cups grated apples, unpeeled
>1 teaspoon vanilla
>½ cup chopped nuts
>1 cup flour
>1 teaspoon cinnamon
>1 teaspoon baking powder
>½ teaspoon baking soda
>¼ teaspoon salt
>Caramel Icing (page 84)

Beat the egg. Add the sugar, oil, grated apples, vanilla, and nuts. Stir in the sifted dry ingredients. Smooth into an 8" x 8" pan and bake at 350°F for about 30 minutes — or until done. With Caramel Icing, it is scrumptious, a complete dessert.

COMPROMISE CAKE
8" x 8"

The only compromising thing about this cake is that, having made it, you'll be asked to make it again and again.

>Rind of 1 orange
>1 cup raisins
>2 cups flour
>½ cup shortening
>½ cup white sugar
>⅔ cup brown sugar
>2 eggs, separated
>1 cup buttermilk
>1 teaspoon baking soda
>½ teaspoon salt

½ cup walnuts or pecans
Orange Butter Icing (page 76) or Penuche Icing
    (page 84)

Put orange rind and raisins through food chopper — or blender
— until very fine. Mix a small amount of the flour with the
fruit. Cream the shortening, add the sugars and blend well. Add
egg yolks and beat well. Add alternately the buttermilk and
remainder of flour sifted with baking soda and salt. Stir in the
raisins, orange rind, and nuts. Fold in the stiffly beaten egg
whites. Turn into a greased 8" x 8" pan. Bake in a 350°F oven
about 55 minutes. When cool, frost with Orange Butter Icing or
with Penuche — for me there's nothing as good as Penuche
Icing.

EPPEL DUNKES KUCHA
(Dunking Apple Cake)
8" x 10"

Tastes good, stays moist — you wouldn't need to dunk it.

½ cup butter
1 cup sugar
1 egg
1 cup warm applesauce
2 cups flour
1 teaspoon baking soda
1 teaspoon cinnamon
½ teaspoon salt
½ teaspoon cloves
1 cup raisins
¾ cup chopped walnuts (optional)
Toasted Coconut Frosting (page 77)

Soften the butter, add the sugar and egg and blend well. Stir in
the applesauce. Sift the dry ingredients and to them add the
raisins and walnuts. Stir into the first mixture. Pour into a
greased oblong cake pan and bake at 350°F for about 40 or 45
minutes. I like mine iced with Toasted Coconut Frosting.

ELSIE'S ORANGE WACKY CAKE
8" x 8"

This is an emergency number. I made it one evening when two friends called to say they'd be with me in less than an hour. Warm from the oven, it was so good we ate the whole cake.

> **1½ cups flour**
> **1 teaspoon baking soda**
> **½ cup brown sugar**
> **½ cup white sugar**
> **½ teaspoon salt**
> **½ teaspoon cinnamon**
> **½ teaspoon nutmeg**
> **½ cup vegetable oil**
> **1 tablespoon vinegar**
> **1 teaspoon vanilla**
> **Grated rind of 1 orange**
> **¾ to 1 cup buttermilk**
>
> *Topping:*
> **½ cup butter at room temperature**
> **⅔ cup brown sugar**
> **½ teaspoon vanilla**
> **⅔ cup flaked coconut**
> **½ cup finely chopped walnuts**

Sift dry ingredients into a 8" x 8" cake pan. Shake the pan till it levels off. Make 3 hollows in the mixture with a spoon and into one put vegetable oil. Into another, vinegar. Into the third, vanilla and grated rind. Over all, pour buttermilk. Stir with a fork until the ingredients are just blended, no more. Clean up any bits of batter on the sides of the pan above the batter level. Bake at 350°F for about 30 minutes, or until the cake springs back when lightly touched.

Meanwhile combine topping ingredients. As soon as the cake is baked, take it from the oven. Spread the topping over it as evenly as you can, and put the cake under the broiler for 2 or 3 minutes till the topping is bubbly and golden. Watch it like a hawk. Cool in the pan on a wire rack. If you can serve it slightly warm, you won't have to worry about storing it.

BANANA CARROT CAKE
9" x 9"

Or should it be called Carrot Banana cake? A frozen banana does very well for this moist, tender delicious cake. Try it and see.

1 cup grated carrots — you don't have to peel them after you wash them
1 banana
1 cup sugar
½ teaspoon salt
½ cup vegetable oil
2 eggs
1¼ cups flour
1 teaspoon baking powder
1 teaspoon baking soda
1 teaspoon cinnamon

Icing:

2 to 3 tablespoons butter
⅔ cup brown sugar
Cream or milk
Nut pieces

After grating the carrots and frozen banana in a food processor, change to the cutting blade and put in all the rest in the order given. If you don't have a processor, mix in the order given. Then pour the batter into a 9" x 9" pan and bake at 350°F for about 35 minutes. To top it off, melt butter; add brown sugar, and enough cream or milk to moisten. Spread it over the cake which you have sprinkled with nut pieces. Put it under the broiler till it bubbles. Or use another icing of your choice.

FRUIT COCKTAIL CAKE
8" x 8"

At a family reunion, one of the cousins — Helen MacPherson — brought a cake that disappeared in no time.

 1 can fruit cocktail
 1 egg
 1½ cups flour
 1 cup sugar
 1 teaspoon baking soda
 1 teaspoon salt

Topping:
 ⅓ cup brown sugar
 ¼ cup chopped nuts
 1 tablespoon flour
 ½ teaspoon cinnamon

Drain the fruit cocktail. You should have about ⅔ cup of fruit syrup. To the syrup, add the egg and beat well. Sift together the flour, sugar, baking soda, and salt. Make a well in the centre of the dry ingredients and add the syrup-egg mixture all at once. Stir only until mixed; don't beat. Fold in the fruit, then pour into an 8" x 8" pan. Mix topping ingredients. Sprinkle over the cake batter. Bake at 375°F for about 45 minutes, or until a toothpick inserted in the centre comes out clean. Cool in the pan.

CHERRY CAKE
9" x 9"

This cake, when prettily iced, makes a delicious dessert.

 ½ cup butter
 1 cup sugar
 2 eggs, separated
 ½ cup milk
 2 cups flour
 1½ teaspoons baking powder
 ½ teaspoon salt

1 cup maraschino cherries, cut in halves
2 tablespoons maraschino cherry juice
Whipped cream or Basic Butter Icing (page 75)

Cream the butter; add the sugar gradually, then the yolks of the eggs, well beaten, the milk and the dry ingredients, mixed and sifted. Fold in the stiffly beaten whites of eggs; add the cherries and juice and bake in a 350°F oven for about an hour. (You can cut down on the cherries, if you think a cupful is too great an extravagance.) Slather at the last minute before serving with whipped cream, or ice it with a butter icing.

UPSA-DAISY CAKE

This one is from the Lutheran Ladies' Aid cookbook. It's tried and true.

4 tablespoons butter
3 tablespoons sherry (may be omitted)
1 cup brown sugar
8 to 12 pitted, cooked, large prunes
12 walnut halves
3 eggs, separated
¼ teaspoon salt
1 cup sugar
½ teaspoon vanilla
½ cup hot water
1 cup sifted cake flour
1 teaspoon baking powder
Whipped cream

Melt the butter in a round cake pan. Add sherry; spread brown sugar evenly over bottom. Arrange prunes and nuts over sugar. Set aside. To egg whites add salt; beat until stiff. Gradually beat in ½ cup of the sugar. Using same beater, beat yolks very light; gradually beat in remaining sugar, vanilla, and hot water. Add flour sifted with baking powder and beat smooth. Fold in egg whites, pour over prunes in pan, and bake in a 325°F oven for about 40 minutes. Invert on a large plate: serve warm, with whipped cream.

KINDERKOCHFEST

Every Oktoberfest from 1970 to 1985, the Waterloo Regional Board of Education and J.M. Schneider Inc. sponsored a Kinderkochfest Competition for all grade 7 and 8 pupils and home economics students of all the collegiates in Waterloo Region. Entries had to fit into one of five categories: salads and hors-d'oeuvres, Black Forest cakes and tortes, pastry and cookies, breads, and specialty German cakes. Nothing could be made with processed foods or mixes. The winners of each category — junior and senior — were given a plaque to take home and one for their school to keep for a year.

Local dignitaries and members of the media and of some German clubs were the judges. Because I'd written a cookbook, I was always invited. The long makeshift tables of fancily iced cakes, tortes, and other delicacies — and some not so delicate — were a mouth-watering sight until one had conscientiously tasted — as I did one year — thirty-two Black Forest cakes.

I was given permission to collect prize-winning recipes — but I have never made the Black Forest cake.

HEIDELBEER BLITZKUCHEN
(BLUEBERRY LIGHTNING CAKE)
8" x 8"

In the Kinderkochfest this cake hadn't risen very high, looked rather funereal and it did not win a prize. But it had good flavour; it was made by a small boy in Grade 7. The cake might not look so sad if you used a fruit that wasn't purple.

> **1 egg**
> **½ cup sugar**
> **¼ cup milk**
> **¼ cup melted butter or margarine**
> **1½ cups flour**
> **2½ teaspoons baking powder**
> **½ teaspoon salt**
>
> *Topping:*
> **2 cups blueberries**
> **⅓ cup sugar**

Beat egg until light. Gradually add ½ cup sugar, then the milk and melted butter. Mix well. Stir in the flour, baking powder, and salt sifted together, blending well. Put in a buttered 8" x 8" pan, then spread blueberries over the dough and sprinkle ⅓ cup sugar over the berries. Bake at 350°F for about 40 minutes.

RHUBARB UPSIDE-DOWN CAKE
9" x 9"

This is a pretty dessert cake. The recipe was sent to me by Joan Picard, who paints pictures, teaches school, and writes poetry.

3 cups rhubarb chunks
10 large marshmallows, cut in half
Strawberries (for colour)
¾ cup sugar

Batter:
½ cup shortening
1 cup sugar
2 eggs
Rind of 1 orange, finely chopped
1¾ cups flour
1 tablespoon baking powder
¼ teaspoon salt
½ cup milk
1 teaspoon almond flavouring

Arrange rhubarb, marshmallows, and strawberries in bottom of a well-buttered iron skillet or a 9" x 9" cake pan. Sprinkle sugar over fruit. To make the batter, cream shortening and sugar. Beat in the eggs one at a time. Add rind. Sift together the dry ingredients and add alternately with the milk and flavouring. Beat until smooth. Spread batter over the rhubarb. Bake at 350°F for 40 to 50 minutes, or until golden brown. Cool for 5 minutes, then loosen the edge of the cake all around with a knife and invert over a serving plate. If you're hesitant to turn it upside down — as I am — cut the cake into serving pieces in the pan. Serve warm with whipped or ice cream. Then write a poem about it. It's worth it.

UPSIDE-DOWN CAKE
9" x 9"

Fruity, luscious and dripping with taffy; vary it with any fruit you like.

½ cup butter or margarine
1½ cups sugar
2 eggs, beaten
2¼ cups flour
½ teaspoon salt
2 teaspoons baking powder
1 cup milk
1 teaspoon vanilla

Upside-down topping:
⅓ cup butter
¾ cup brown sugar
Fruit to cover bottom of cake pan

Cream butter and add sugar gradually. Add eggs and beat until the mixture is fluffy. Sift flour, salt, and baking powder and add alternately with milk and vanilla, beating well after each addition. If you want a good, white, foolproof, moist, plain cake, you can stop right there; put it into a square pan and bake it at 350°F for 45 minutes. But if you want to take a chance on making a super-dessert; melt ⅓ cup butter in a 9" x 9" pan, sprinkle ¾ cup brown sugar evenly over the butter and arrange drained fruit in an attractive pattern on the butter-sugar base. You might try pineapple rounds with maraschino cherries and pecan halves, or large pitted prunes with walnut halves, peach or apricot halves, canned or raw, with cherries or blanched almonds, or apple slices, blueberries (even raspberries, though they are rather soft). Bake at 350°F for 45 minutes. Turn the cake upside-down and remove pan while it is hot. Patch up the fruity part if it needs patching. Serve it as soon as it's cool enough, with or without whipped cream or ice cream.

Warning: Once I made a pineapple upside-down cake for a Spin-the-Wheel booth at a Rotary Carnival. Winners always chose the mile-high, eye-appealing, professionally-iced sponge cakes (dry as dust in the midriff, I'm sure) and left my luscious but flatter offering on the shelf.

EASY RHUBARB UPSIDE-DOWN CAKE
9" x 9"

This is an easy dessert.

¼ cup butter
4 to 5 cups diced rhubarb
1 cup brown sugar

Turn on your oven to 350°F. Melt the butter in a 9" x 9" baking pan, add the diced rhubarb and sugar mixed together and spread over the butter, covering the bottom of the pan. If you are using frozen rhubarb, put it in the oven to thaw while you mix up the batter.

Batter:
1 cup sugar
1½ cups flour
2 teaspoons baking powder
½ teaspoon salt
¼ cup shortening
1 egg
1 teaspoon vanilla
About ⅔ cup milk

Sift the sugar, flour, baking powder, and salt. Add the soft shortening and cut it into the flour mixture. Beat up the egg in a cup, stir in the vanilla and fill the cup with milk, beating all together; pour the liquid over the flour mixture and blend till smooth. Spread the batter over the rhubarb evenly. Bake at 350°F for about 30 to 40 minutes until the cake tests done. It will be light as a feather, delicious; serve warm with a scoop of vanilla ice cream. Don't turn it upside down on a plate — simply cut it in squares and lift out each square with a pancake turner and plop it rhubarb-side-up on a serving plate.

If you want a Rhubarb Upside-Down Gingerbread Cake, add ½ teaspoon each of cinnamon, nutmeg, ginger, and ½ cup of molasses instead of half the sugar.

LARGER CAKES

Mother loved cake; she'd eat it for breakfast, dinner, and supper. "No use letting it get stale," she'd explain, but as soon as a cake was all gone she'd say, "I haven't a cake in the house," and immediately bake another one.

In Bevvy's household, a cake seldom lasts a day; then Salome stirs up another from the many recipes in Bevvy's little black book where only the ingredients are listed.

In interpreting Bevvy's and Mother's recipes here, I've suggested standard directions. I've tried many of them and they work — almost always. When I bake a cake, I believe in being precise about things like baking soda and baking powder, and fairly accurate about proportions of liquid and dry, but I can't imagine messily measuring three tablespoons of butter when it's so easy to simply slice a sliver off the pound.

What if a cake doesn't come out of the oven high and light as a piece of foam rubber or a cake mix? You might be the best meat-cooker and potato-boiler in the world, but you know it's the person who turns out those cakes with the fluffy pink icing sprinkled with little silver balls and multicoloured doodads that gets all the praise.

I've shied away from Bevvy's recipes that call for more than three eggs; those Mennonite farmers' wives with whom she swapped her recipes didn't have to economize, they just went into the chicken pen, pulled an old hen off the nest and found half a dozen eggs they could cheerfully break into a batter. For a reason other than economy, I've also eliminated recipes that call for cupfuls of cream.

BANANA CAKE
9" x 13"

I've tried a lot of banana cake recipes and I'm sure this is the best. It stays moist, and with a penuche icing it's out of this world.

½ cup soft shortening
1½ cups sugar
2 large eggs
2¼ cups flour
1 teaspoon baking powder
¾ teaspoon baking soda
1 teaspoon salt
¼ cup buttermilk
1 cup mashed ripe bananas
½ cup chopped walnuts or pecans
Whipped cream and sliced bananas *OR*
Penuche Icing (page 84)

Cream together until fluffy the shortening and sugar; beat in thoroughly the eggs. Sift together the dry ingredients and stir them in alternately with the milk, banana, and nuts. Pour into a greased and floured 9" x 13" cake pan, or two layer-pans; bake at 350°F until the cake tests done — about 25 to 30 minutes for the layers, 40 to 45 for the long pan. For the layer cake, you can spread whipped cream and sliced bananas for a filling and slather whipped cream over the top with slices of banana round the edges — a scrumptious company dessert. If you're making it in the long pan, ice it with Penuche. I'd even favour icing the layers with Penuche Icing.

NORM'S CHOCOLATE OATMEAL CAKE
8" x 13"

Norm is a great cake baker; when she gave me this recipe I could hardly wait to get at it.

> 1½ cups boiling water
> 1 cup rolled oats
> ½ cup shortening (Norm uses butter melted
>   to bubbling)
> 1½ cups sugar
> 2 eggs
> 1 cup flour
> ½ cup cocoa
> 1 teaspooon baking soda
> ½ teaspoon salt
> 1 teaspooon vanilla
> Cocoa Fudge Icing (page 81)

Pour boiling water over oats and let stand until cool. Cream shortening with sugar and eggs, add the cooled oats and the rest (except icing). Beat until smooth. Bake in an 8" x 13" pan at 350°F for 35 minutes. Norm ices this with Cocoa Fudge Icing.

MOCHA CHOCOLATE CAKE
8" x 11"

With orange peel added in little chunks, this is one of the best cakes of my life.

> ⅔ cup butter or margarine at room temperature
> 2 cups brown sugar
> ½ cup cocoa
> 1 egg
> Rind of 2 oranges, chopped about the size of a
>   dime (not grated)
> 1 cup buttermilk
> 1 teaspooon vanilla
> 2 teaspoons instant coffee
> ¾ cup hot water
> 2½ cups flour

2 teaspoons baking powder
1 teaspooon baking soda
Salt to taste (or none)
Boiled Chocolate Icing (page 81)

Cream butter with blended sugar and cocoa. Add egg and the orange rind. Stir in milk and vanilla. Dissolve the coffee in the hot water and add to batter. Sift together flour, baking powder, baking soda, and salt. Add all at once to batter. Mix well, then pour into an 8" x 11" Pyrex pan and bake at 325°F for 30 to 35 minutes, or until a toothpick inserted in centre comes out clean. Slathered with glossy Boiled Chocolate Icing, using 1 teaspoon of an orange liqueur instead of vanilla, this cake will disappear like snow in spring sunshine.

FEATHER-LIGHT CHOCOLATE CAKE
8" x 13"

This is fun and very easy to make. It's also big — but don't let that deceive you: everyone will want a second or third piece.

2 cups flour
2 cups sugar
½ cup vegetable oil
¼ cup butter or margarine
4 slightly rounded tablespoons cocoa
1 cup water
½ cup buttermilk
2 eggs, lightly beaten
1 teaspooon vanilla
1 teaspooon baking soda
Boiled Chocolate Icing (page 81)

In a large bowl, sift together the flour and sugar. In a saucepan over medium heat, combine the oil, butter, cocoa, and water. Bring to a boil, stirring constantly. Pour over the flour-sugar mixture. Add buttermilk, eggs, and vanilla. Sprinkle the baking soda over all and beat well. Pour into an ungreased 8" x 13" pan. Bake at 400°F for 15 to 20 minutes, or until a toothpick inserted in the centre comes out clean. When cool, ice and serve.

OATMEAL CAKE
(from Mrs. Ammon Bauman)
9" x 11"

Moist and marvellous, with a crispy, delicious icing baked on.

1⅓ cups boiling water
1 cup quick rolled oats
½ cup butter
1 cup brown sugar
1 cup white sugar
2 eggs,beaten
1⅓ cups flour
1 teaspooon baking soda
1 teaspoon cinnamon
1 teaspooon salt

Pour boiling water over the oats, stir and let cool. Cream together the butter and sugars, then add the eggs beaten till fluffy. Sift the dry ingredients and add them alternately with the soaked oatmeal until blended. Turn into a buttered 9" x 11" pan, bake at 350°F for about 35 minutes.

While the cake is baking, mix the topping:

6 tablespoons melted butter
½ cup brown sugar
½ cup dessicated coconut
½ cup coarsely chopped nuts
¼ cup cream
½ teaspoon vanilla

While the cake is hot, carefully spread the topping over it smoothly. Broil 4 inches from the burner until just melted and bubbly, watching it all the time. Oh, boy!

1-2-3-4 CAKE
9" x 13"

This was Mother's most fool-proof light cake.

1 cup butter
2 cups sugar
3 cups flour
4 eggs
2 teaspoons cream of tartar
1 teaspoon baking soda
1 cup cold water or milk
1 teaspoon vanilla

Cream butter, add sugar and blend, beat in the eggs; sift the flour, cream of tartar, and baking soda twice before adding to the batter alternately with the milk and vanilla. (Put in a cup of raisins or walnuts for variety.) Pour into a buttered and floured 9" x 13" cake pan or two layer pans, and bake in 350°F oven: 45 minutes for the large cake pan, 30 for the layer pans. Test it.

Mother usually iced it with a Basic Butter Icing, but sometimes, glory of glories, she made Mocha Cakes.

MOCHA CAKES

These were Mother's pride and joy. To this day people who came to parties at our house sixty years ago say to me, "I remember those marvellous Mocha Cakes your mother used to make."

When Mother's 1-2-3-4 cake in a large pan was completely cold, she would cut it in 2-inch squares, each of which she would carefully ice, top and sides, with a rich **butter icing** (page 75). Immediately, before the icing could set, she would dip the cake on all sides into very **finely chopped almonds** which she had previously browned in **butter**. You never tasted such cakes. A lot of bother, mind you, blanching and hand-chopping, and buttering all those nuts — but think of enjoying a deserved reputation for doing it throughout all those years.

INGENUITY

One day when Lorna and Ross were coming for dinner, I tried a recipe for a cake that had lots of nuts in it. After the prescribed time, I opened the oven door to have a look and was surprised to see that the cake hadn't risen. It was flat and golden and rich, but it wasn't a cake. I wondered why until I opened my flour drawer to get flour for thickening the gravy, and there I saw the sifter full of flour that I'd forgotten to put in the cake! How could such a stupid thing happen? Kath was visiting from Devon and we had been talking, talking, talking.

There was no time to make another dessert. I cut the rich concoction into squares, put one on each serving plate, topped it with ice cream and it was enjoyed by all. We even had second helpings. Not to waste what was left, I gave it a whirl in my food processor and used it as a nutty crumb topping on another dessert later on.

SPICE AND WALNUT CAKE
9" x 13"

This big, flat, flavourful cake is easy to make and stays moist.

> **1 cup shortening**
> **1½ cups brown sugar**
> **½ cup white sugar**
> **2 eggs**
> **1 teaspooon vanilla**
> **2½ cups flour**
> **1 teaspoon baking soda**
> **1 teaspoon salt**
> **½ teaspoon nutmeg**
> **½ teaspoon allspice**
> **½ teaspoon cinnamon**
> **1¼ cups buttermilk**
> **1 cup chopped walnuts**

Cream shortening. Add sugars and blend well; beat in eggs and vanilla. Sift together the flour, baking soda, salt, nutmeg, allspice, and cinnamon. Add flour mixture and buttermilk alternately to the butter-sugar mixture; then stir in walnuts. Pour batter into a buttered 9" x 13" pan. Bake at 350°F for 40 to 45 minutes, or until a toothpick inserted in centre of cake comes out clean. Cool on a rack in the pan.

MATTIE BEARINGER'S MAPLE SYRUP CAKE
8" x 13"

Two layers or a big one, sweet and light, you can stir it up in a hurry.

½ **cup butter or margarine**
¼ **cup sugar**
2 **eggs**
1 **cup maple syrup**
2¼ **cups flour**
1 **tablespoon baking powder**
¾ **teaspoon baking soda**
¼ **teaspoon ginger**
½ **teaspoon salt**
½ **cup hot water**
Soft Maple Icing (page 76)

Beat the butter and sugar until light and creamy; add the eggs one at a time, beating well after each one. Blend in the maple syrup gradually. Add the sifted dry ingredients alternately with the hot water: 3 additions of dry, 2 of water. Blend well, then spread batter evenly into an 8" x 13" pan or two 8-inch layer pans. Bake at 350°F for 45 minutes for the large pan, 25 to 30 for the layers. Cool on a wire rack. Fill and frost.

EGGLESS, BUTTERLESS, AND MILKLESS CAKE
9" x 13"

This is fun to make, and everyone who came to my house had a second serving and might have had more but unfortunately by that time it was all gone. The recipe came from a cookbook published in 1917 during the First World War when cooks had to skimp. There were two recipes in the book with the same title but slightly different ingredients. One called for 2 tablespoons of lard, the other a cupful of shortening. I compromised by using ½ cup margarine. In the 1917 book there were no further directions; I baked my cake in a 350°F oven for about 40 minutes, when it tested done. Served slightly warm it has great flavour. It keeps well, too, because of the raisins.

> **2 cups sugar**
> **2 cups water**
> **½ cup shortening**
> **2 cups raisins**
> **1 teaspoon cinnamon**
> **3 cups flour**
> **1 teaspoon baking powder**
> **½ teaspoon baking soda**
> **½ teaspoon nutmeg**
> **½ teaspoon ground cloves**

Into a saucepan, measure sugar, water, shortening, and raisins. Boil for 4 minutes. Cool. Sift together and add remaining ingredients. Bake at 350°F for 40 minutes.

DRIED APPLE SCHNITZ

Every autumn Eva spends days peeling, coring, and schnitzing (slicing) apples: she spreads the apple segments on pans in the oven and on top of her big black wood-stove. When they are thoroughly dry and crisp, she stores them in sacks in an upstairs room where they'll keep for months, becoming spongey and chewy.

"And how do you use them?" I asked her.

"We used to cook them with prunes — schnitz and gwetcha — and have them on the table every day for breakfast." She smiled. "Now I pack them in plastic bags and sell them at the Waterloo market to the university students. They're crazy for them as snacks." Eva brought me her handwritten cookbook. "Lovina sometimes makes dried schnitz into a really good cake." I copied the recipe.

SCHNITZ or FARMERS' FRUIT CAKE
9" x 13"

I could hardly wait to try it — with some of Eva's dried schnitz. The cake was divine — big, rich, moist and with that elusive old-fashioned flavour.

2 cups dried apple schnitz
2 cups molasses
1 cup butter or lard
2 cups brown sugar
2 eggs, well beaten
1 cup buttermilk
4 cups flour
1 teaspoon cinnamon
1 teaspoon allspice
½ teaspoon nutmeg
2 teaspoons baking soda

Soak the apples overnight in water. In the morning drain them and put them through a food chopper (or processor). Simmer the apples in the molasses with the butter for an hour. "If you don't put the butter in, the apples will form into a hard taffy ball," Eva told me. When the apples have cooled, add the brown sugar, well-beaten eggs, buttermilk, flour, spices, and baking soda. Pour into a 9" x 13" pan and bake at 350°F for an hour. Test it with a toothpick. The top is crusty and chewy and doesn't need icing which might detract from the fantastic flavour.

HAPPY APPLE CAKE
9" x 13"

This is one of the best. Light and moist, it keeps well — if you can resist temptation long enough to let it.

**2 eggs
2 cups sugar
1 cup vegetable oil
3 cups flour
1 teaspoon baking soda
½ teaspoon salt
3 cups cored and chopped apples
2 teaspoons vanilla
½ cup chopped nuts
½ cup buttermilk**

Frosting:
**1 cup brown sugar
¼ cup milk
¼ cup butter**

Beat eggs, sugar, and oil. Sift together and add flour, baking soda, and salt. Stir in apples, vanilla, nuts, and buttermilk. Mix well. Smooth into a 9" x 13" pan. Bake at 350°F for about 40 minutes. Cool in the pan. When still warm, boil frosting ingredients for 2 minutes. Do not beat. Drizzle over baked cake while warm.

APPLESAUCE FRUIT CAKE
8" x 13" or thereabout

Mary Garwood is a decorator but she knows how to make the lightest fruity cake that any of her winter friends in Arizona ever tasted.

**2 cups flour
1 teaspoon baking soda
½ teaspoon salt
½ teaspoon cinnamon
½ teaspoon ground cloves**

½ teaspoon nutmeg
½ teaspoon allspice
2 tablespoons cocoa
½ cup soft shortening
1½ cups sugar
2 eggs
¾ cup snipped pitted dates
¾ cup chopped walnuts
¾ cup seedless raisins
1½ cups applesauce
Mocha Icing (page 82)

Sift together the flour, baking soda, salt, spices, and cocoa. In another bowl, blend the shortening and sugar, beating in the eggs one at a time till fluffy; stir the cut-up dates, walnuts, and raisins into the flour mixture and blend into the egg mixture alternately with the applesauce until the batter is smooth. Pour into a greased pan about 8" x 13" and bake at 350°F for 55 to 60 minutes. Let cool and ice with Mocha Icing.

CRUSHED PINEAPPLE CAKE
9" x 13"

Here's what you can do with one of those tins of pineapple that were on sale at the supermarket. You'll probably buy another tin after you've tasted this.

2 cups sugar
2 eggs
2 cups flour
2 teaspoons baking soda
Salt
1 can crushed pineapple, undrained
1 teaspoon vanilla
½ cup chopped pecans or walnuts

Beat sugar and eggs until fluffy. Sift flour, baking soda, and salt, and stir into the egg mixture. Blend in the pineapple, vanilla, and nuts. Pour into a 9" x 13" pan and bake at 350°F for about 40 to 45 minutes or till it stops singing.

CHOCOLATE ZUCCHINI CAKE
7" x 10"

Soft, tender, tasty. With the help of my food processor I had this cake in the oven in a few minutes when I was expecting company for tea. Everybody ate three squares and kept saying, "That's good!"

2 eggs
¾ cup vegetable oil
1 cup sugar
1 teaspoon salt
1 teaspoon vanilla
1 cup flour
1 teaspoon baking soda
1 teaspoon cinnamon
3 tablespoons cocoa
1½ cups grated zucchini
½ cup chopped nuts
Cream Cheese Icing (page 45)

Beat the eggs, oil, sugar, salt, and vanilla until well blended. Sift flour, baking soda, cinnamon, and cocoa, and mix well with the egg-sugar combination until smooth. Stir in the zucchini and nuts. Pour into a cake pan about 7" x 10" and bake at 350°F for 20 to 30 minutes, or until a toothpick inserted in the centre comes out clean. Frost with Cream Cheese Icing if you like. I prefer serving it slightly warm from the oven and without icing.

ZUCCHINI SPICE CAKE
9" x 13" or thereabout

Norm said this was the best-tasting cake she'd ever eaten at my
house: moist and heavy, in the East European tradition, it
would probably keep well but never lasts long enough to be
tested.

> 1 cup white sugar
> 1 cup brown sugar
> 2½ cups flour
> 2 teaspoons baking soda
> 1 teaspoon baking powder
> 1 tablespoon cinnamon
> 1 teaspoon ginger
> ½ teaspoon cloves
> 1 teaspoon salt
> 1 cup vegetable oil
> 1 tablespoon vanilla
> 3 eggs
> 2 cups grated, unpeeled zucchini
> 1 cup raisins
> 1 cup chopped walnuts
> 2 tablespoons grated orange rind

Into a fairly large bowl, measure the sugars, flour, baking soda,
baking powder, spices, and salt, sifted together. Pour in the oil,
add the vanilla and break in the eggs; beat all together till well
blended. Stir in the zucchini, raisins, nuts, and orange rind. Pour
into a 9" x 13" pan and bake in a 350°F oven for 45 to 50 minutes.
Cool in the pan on a rack.

ROSY RHUBARB CAKE
9" x 13"

This is an attractive dessert, besides being tasty. It makes quite a few pieces but does not serve many people because everyone will want several helpings.

Batter:
¼ cup butter
½ cup sugar
½ teaspoon salt
1 egg
1 cup milk
2 cups flour
2 teaspoons baking powder
4 cups sliced rhubarb
3 tablespoons strawberry or raspberry Jell-o powder

Topping:
1 cup brown sugar
½ teaspoon cinnamon
½ cup flour
½ cup rolled oats
¼ cup butter

Cream butter, sugar, and salt. Beat in egg. Alternately add the milk and the flour sifted with the baking powder. Pour the batter into a 9" x 13" pan. Spread the rhubarb pieces evenly over batter; sprinkle the Jell-o powder over the rhubarb. Blend the topping ingredients and spread over the rhubarb. Bake at 375°F for 30 to 40 minutes, or until a toothpick inserted in the centre comes out clean. Cut into squares and serve warm or cool with whipped cream or ice cream if you want to be fancy. You needn't be, it's good enough without.

LAYER CAKES

Birthdays, weddings, Christmases, Oktoberfest — all have their special cakes. In my house, a cake is baked only when enough people are coming to eat it while it is fresh. If a whole cake isn't eaten at once, I will finish it myself — to the detriment of what little figure I have left. (Of course I could freeze the remainder.)

Mother always had a cake in the house. As soon as we finished eating one, she'd bake another. With five of us to enjoy them, cakes didn't last long.

I don't bake as many cakes as I used to — not since I discovered that coffee cakes, muffins, and quick breads are easier to make and to serve company with afternoon tea. I do still make the little 8" x 8" cakes that I can stir up in a hurry with a baked-on topping or put under the broiler. It's those big, glamorous, sticky cakes that are the problem.

For me, the high, round, special-occasion cakes are a dessert to be served with ice cream or — if they are really fancy, like a Black Forest cake or a torte — smothered with whipped cream.

I read somewhere that cakes are delicately balanced formulas and that cake baking is an exacting art. You have to follow directions; you can't have fun substituting other ingredients without risking disaster. You might get away with it in the small ones, but don't take chances with a glamorous creation for a celebration.

SCHWARZWAELDER KIRSCHTORTE
(Black Forest Cherry Torte)

The winner of the Black Forest Cake category in the Kinderkochfest was made from a recipe that was very long and complicated. When my Hilda made the Black Forest Torte she was so proud of it, it took her almost a day. This version is simpler.

1½ cups whipping cream
3 eggs, well beaten
1 teaspoon vanilla
2 cups flour
3 tablespoons cocoa
1½ cups sugar
2 teaspoons baking powder
½ teaspoon salt

Cherry Filling:
1 can whole cherries or equivalent
2 teaspoons cornstarch
1 tablespoon sugar
1 teaspoon Kirsch or brandy
2 cups whipping cream
½ cup icing sugar
Chocolate curls

Whip the cream until stiff; fold in the eggs and vanilla. Sift together flour, cocoa, sugar, baking powder, and salt. Fold gently into the egg mixture. Spread in 2 buttered and floured 9-inch cake pans. Bake at 350°F for 30 to 35 minutes. Remove carefully from pans. Cool, then fill and decorate.

To make filling: drain cherries reserving juice. In a saucepan, mix cornstarch and sugar. Add water to reserved juice to equal 1 cup. Stir into cornstarch mixture and cook over medium heat until clear. Cool to lukewarm, add Kirsch. Fold cherries into sauce and cool completely. Whip the 2 cups of cream, gradually adding icing sugar, until stiff. Form a rim of cream around the edge of cake layer; fill centre with half of cherry filling. Put another layer of cake on top and do the same with it. Finally, slather the whole cake, sides and top, with whipped cream. Decorate with chocolate curls.

CARROT CAKE

Wende Gregory, the darling bride who worked in Kitchener's Provident Mennonite book store where you could browse, sit in front of a charming real fireplace, and have a free cup of coffee, gave me her favourite cake recipe. "I don't call it carrot cake because people don't want to even taste it then. I call it Wednesday cake or whatever day of the week I baked it on," she told me.

2 cups sugar
2 cups flour
2 teaspoons baking soda
2 teaspoons cinnamon
Pinch of salt
1¼ cups vegetable oil
4 eggs
3 cups finely shredded carrots
2 teaspoons vanilla

Mix dry ingredients together. Blend in oil, add eggs and carrots, then vanilla. Blend well and bake in two 8-inch round pans at 350°F for 35 minutes.

Icing:
1 package cream cheese
½ cup butter
3½ cups icing sugar
1 teaspoon vanilla
1 teaspoon orange juice
1 cup finely chopped pecans

Blend cheese and butter, slowly add sugar, vanilla, orange juice, and nuts. Ice only after cake is completely cold.

This cake is very moist and delicious and can easily be halved if you don't want a layer cake.

Since this recipe was published in *Food That Really Schmecks*, I've been told by several people that they've added raisins and baked it for a wedding cake.

SCHOKOLADEN SCHICHTKUCHEN

A Grade 7 boy made this fudge layer cake for the Kinderkoch-fest. I made it for Patti's fourteenth birthday dinner and every-one ate two big pieces.

> 2 cups flour
> 1 teaspoon baking soda
> 1 teaspoon salt
> ½ cup cocoa
> 2 cups brown sugar, packed
> ½ cup shortening, butter, or margarine
> 1 cup buttermilk
> 1 teaspoon vanilla
> 3 unbeaten eggs
> Super Chocolate Chip Icing (page 79)

Sift the flour, baking soda, salt, and cocoa into a mixing bowl; add the sugar, shortening, buttermilk, and vanilla and beat for 2 minutes. Add the eggs one at a time and beat another 2 minutes. Pour the batter into two 8-inch round pans and bake for 30 minutes in a 350°F oven. (If you want a big oblong cake, 9" x 13", bake for 40 to 45 minutes.) Invert layers on a rack to cool.

I used Lorna's Super Chocolate Chip Icing to cover both lay-ers, lit the candles on top and we sang, "Happy birthday, dear Patti."

ALEDA BAUMAN'S SPEEDY CHOCOLATE CAKE

If you have a mixer, you can whack this together in minutes; if not, your right arm can do it. The result is tender, tasty, moist, with a fine texture.

> 1½ cups flour
> 1¼ cups sugar
> 1 cup buttermilk
> ½ cup cocoa
> ⅔ cup vegetable oil

2 eggs
1¼ teaspoons baking soda
1 teaspoon vanilla
1 teaspoon salt

Blend all the ingredients till moistened then beat at medium speed for 3 minutes. That's it. Pour the batter into two 8-inch round layer pans or into a 9" x 13" pan — if you want your cake to be about 3 inches high. Bake the layers at 350°F for about 25 to 30 minutes and the square one about 5 minutes longer. Test with a toothpick. Ice with whatever you like. I, being lazy or in a hurry, usually make the square cake and spread over it a mixture of **1 cup brown sugar**, **¼ cup butter**, and **a handful chopped walnuts** as soon as it comes out of the oven. Then I pop it back in again under the broiler for about 1 or 2 minutes and watch it like a cat.

GEBURTSTAG KUCHA
(Birthday Cake from Rebecca Weber)

Snow white and light as a feather; baked in layers.

½ cup butter
2 cups sugar
3½ cups flour
3 teaspoons baking powder
1 teaspoon salt
1½ cups ice water
1 teaspoon vanilla
½ teaspoon almond extract
4 egg whites, beaten stiff
Angel Feather Icing (page 80)

Cream butter and sugar until light. Sift dry ingredients and add alternately with ice water and flavourings, beating thoroughly after each addition. Fold in the beaten egg whites. Pour into two greased 8-inch round pans and bake at 350°F for about 30 minutes. Cover with Angel Feather Icing and be tactful about the number of candles.

SAUERKRAUT CHOCOLATE CAKE

Leftover, cooked sauerkraut makes this cake moist and delicious.

⅔ cup butter
1½ cups sugar
3 eggs
1 cup water
2¼ cups flour
½ cup cocoa
1 teaspoon baking powder
1 teaspoon baking soda
½ teaspoon salt
⅔ cup drained sauerkraut
1 teaspoon vanilla
Mocha Icing (page 82)

Blend butter and sugar, beat in the eggs, one at a time; add water alternately with sifted dry ingredients, then stir in the sauerkraut and vanilla. Pour batter into two greased 8-inch round pans and bake in a 350°F oven for 30 minutes. Cool on racks and ice with Mocha Icing. Strangely enough, the cake doesn't taste of sauerkraut.

DEVIL'S FOOD LAYER CAKE

This is a good big one; sometimes you need that kind.

½ cup butter
1 cup white sugar
1 cup brown sugar
2 eggs, separated and beaten
2 squares unsweetened chocolate, melted
3½ cups flour
1 teaspoon baking powder
⅛ teaspoon cinnamon
⅛ teaspoon allspice

1 cup buttermilk
1 teaspoon baking soda
1 teaspoon vanilla
Orange or Date Filling (page 85 or 86)
Soft Chocolate Icing (page 82)

Cream butter and sugars, add egg yolks and melted chocolate. Sift flour, baking powder, and spices, then add to butter mixture alternately with milk in which the baking soda has been dissolved. Add vanilla and fold in the beaten egg whites. Pour into two greased, floured 8-inch round pans and bake in a 350°F oven for 30 minutes. Especially good with Orange or Date Filling between the layers and Soft Chocolate Icing over all.

MAPLE SYRUP CAKE

Two layers of sweetness and light!

½ cup shortening
½ cup sugar
¾ cup maple syrup
2 eggs, beaten
1 teaspoon vanilla
2 cups cake flour
½ teaspoon salt
2½ teaspoons baking powder
½ cup butternuts, walnuts, or pecans
Soft Maple Icing (page 76)

Blend the shortening, sugar, syrup, eggs, and vanilla. Sift the flour, salt, and baking powder, stir in the nuts and add all to the blended mixture. Pour into greased, floured 8-inch round pans and bake at 375°F for 20 minutes. Cool a few minutes then carefully turn cakes onto racks to become cold. Put together with Soft Maple Icing and ice all over.

COCONUT CLOUD CAKE
(from Serena Shantz)

Pretty and good; you can easily cut the recipe in half if you don't want a layer cake, or bake it in a 9" x 13" pan — as I do. I've had people say this recipe alone was worth the cost of my cookbook.

¾ cup butter
1½ cups sugar
3 eggs, separated
3 cups flour
4½ teaspoons baking powder
¾ teaspoon salt
1 cup dessicated coconut
2 cups milk
1 teaspoon vanilla
1 teaspoon almond extract
Angel Feather Icing (page 80)

Cream butter, add sugar and beaten egg yolks and 1 egg white; continue beating. Sift flour with baking powder and salt, mix with coconut and add alternately with milk and flavourings to butter mixture. Pour into two greased 8-inch round pans and bake in 350°F oven for about 30 minutes. Cool; remove from pans to a rack and ice with Angel Feather Icing, sprinkle shredded coconut generously on top and sides of cake after you've iced both the layers and put one on top of the other.

CIDER CAKE

Here's a cake that was perfect; it looked just like a picture and had great flavour as well. I was really proud of it.

½ cup margarine or butter
1½ cups lightly packed brown sugar
2 eggs
2 cups cake flour
2 teaspoons baking powder
¾ teaspoon salt
¼ teaspoon baking soda

½ teaspoon nutmeg
1 teaspoon cinnamon
½ cup milk
½ cup cider
1 cup chopped walnuts
Basic Butter Icing (page 75)
Apple Butter (optional)

Cream the margarine and blend in the brown sugar. Beat in the eggs until the mixture is fluffy. Stir the sifted dry ingredients into the creamed mixture alternately with the milk and cider, making 3 dry and 2 liquid additions, combining lightly after each. Fold in the chopped nuts. Pour into two buttered and floured 8-inch round pans. Bake at 350°F for about 30 to 35 minutes.

Frost with Butter Icing moistened with cider, using apple butter or icing as a filling between the layers.

Five days after I baked this cake, my guests exclaimed how tasty and moist it was. Why did half of it last so long? Because I hid it, that's why.

GRAHAM WAFER CAKE

Mother was thrilled with this very rich, layer-cake recipe.

2 tablespoons butter
1¼ cups sugar
2 eggs
Pinch of salt
1 teaspoon baking soda
32 graham wafers, rolled and sifted
1½ cups buttermilk
Lemon or Cream Filling (pages 86 or 87)
Angel Feather Icing (page 80)

Blend the butter and sugar, beat in the eggs and salt; sift the baking soda with the graham wafers and add alternately with the buttermilk. Pour into two greased 8-inch round pans and bake in a 350°F oven for 30 minutes, or until it tests done. Mother put Lemon or Cream Filling between the layers and iced the cake with Angel Feather Icing.

HONEY WALNUT CAKE
(from Ella Sittler)

This high layer cake is a real show-off, with great flavour and texture, and tanny-gold icing.

¼ cup butter
1½ cups chopped walnuts
¼ cup honey

Batter:
¾ cup butter
1¼ cups sugar
2 eggs
2½ cups flour
1 teaspoon salt
1 teaspoon baking soda
1 cup buttermilk

Honey Nut Frosting:
¼ cup butter
2½ cups brown sugar
¼ cup cream or whole milk
½ cup honey-nut mixture

Melt ¼ cup butter in a cake pan in the oven; spread the walnuts over the butter and drizzle the honey over the nuts. Put the pan in a 350°F oven for 10 minutes, not longer; it will be bubbly. Take it out of the oven and let it cool while you stir up the batter.

Cream ¾ cup butter and 1¼ cups sugar until light. Add the eggs and beat till well blended. Sift the flour, salt, and baking soda together and blend with the egg mixture alternately with the buttermilk.

Remove half a cup of the nut mixture from the cake pan to be used in the icing. Scrape the rest of the nut mixture into the cake batter and fold it in. Pour the batter into two buttered and lightly floured 8-inch round pans. (If you don't want a layer cake, you could put it in the pan you used for the honey-nut mixture.) Bake in a 350°F oven for about 30 minutes for the layers (slightly longer for the deeper pan). Cool in the pans for 10 minutes, then turn out on a wire rack to finish cooling.

Frost each layer with Honey Nut Frosting; put all the ingredients — including the reserved honey-nut mixture — into a pan and bring to a gentle boil for about 2 minutes. Set aside to cool, beat it till it is the right consistency to spread on the cake. You'll get your reward.

GERMAN BEER CAKE

Wendy Ueberschlag, Virginia Mittleholtz, and three of their friends entered this cake in Kinderkochfest.

½ cup soft butter or margarine
1 cup sugar
2 eggs
½ cup molasses
2⅓ cups flour
Pinch of salt
¼ teaspoon cinnamon
¼ teaspoon allspice
¼ teaspoon cloves
2 teaspoons baking powder
¾ cup beer

Frosting:
2 cups icing sugar
2 tablespoons cocoa
3 tablespoons softened butter
3 tablespoons strong coffee
¼ teaspoon vanilla
⅛ teaspoon salt

Cream butter and sugar; add the eggs one at a time, beating after each. Stir in the molasses. Sift the dry ingredients together and add along with the beer to the creamed mixture. Pour batter in two lightly buttered 8-inch cake pans. Bake at 350°F for about 30 minutes, or until toothpick inserted in centre comes out clean. Let cool on racks. Blend all frosting ingredients together. Spread ⅓ on one cooled layer. Place other layer on top and frost top and sides.

CAKES IN A TUBE PAN

Don't be discouraged if whatever you make doesn't look like the glamorous pictures in magazines or gourmet cookbooks; the photographers use all sorts of tricks to get their effects. Whipped cream would melt under hot lights so they use shaving cream. A plump roasted chicken is usually raw or it would appear shrunken; and sometimes photographers use dye or oil to make cakes look good.

NORM'S FAMILY BIRTHDAY CAKE

Every time there is a birthday in our family, Norm makes this super-elegant delicious mocha angel cake. Her grand-daughter, Dr. Patti, lights the candles and we all sing "Happy Birthday" when she carries it to the table. It should serve twelve generously but eight of us have been known to eat all of it.

Norm bakes an angel cake mix the day before the birthday. She keeps it in the pan until next morning, then takes it out. Her husband, Ralph, very carefully slices it horizontally into five layers. Meanwhile Norm makes the mocha filling:

Cream:

> **1 cup margarine**
> **1½ cups icing sugar**

Add:

> **Pinch of salt**
> **1 teaspoon vanilla**
> **2 eggs yolks**

Beat thoroughly and add:

> **¼ cup cocoa (or 2 squares melted unsweetened chocolate)**
> **6 tablespoons double-strength coffee — more or less — to make a spreadable icing.**

Ice the bottom layer of the cake; put next layer on top and ice it, continuing until all the layers have been iced and added. Chill the cake until near serving time then cover generously with whipped cream sweetened with sugar and vanilla. Garnish with candles, light them, and sing lustily in anticipation of the best birthday cake you have ever eaten.

ANGEL CAKE

I have never baked a real angel cake. With a foolproof commercial angel cake mix, I make a tall gorgeous synthetic creation and brazenly enjoy the exclamations that come when I produce it beautifully decorated with Angel Feather Icing (page 80) and birthday candles or sparsely sprinkled with those tiny coloured candy bits.

PURE ANGEL CAKE

Of course, if you want to try the real thing, here is Mother's recipe. Good luck.

1 cup sifted cake flour
1 cup egg whites (9 to 11 eggs)
¼ teaspoon salt
¾ teaspoon cream of tartar
1¼ cups sifted fine granulated sugar
¾ teaspoon vanilla
¼ teaspoon almond flavouring

Sift flour once, measure and sift four more times. Beat egg whites with salt; when foamy, add cream of tartar and continue beating until eggs are stiff enough to hold up in peaks, but not dry. (Mother's recipe says to do this on a large platter with a wire whip or two forks — I hope you have an electric beater.) Fold in the sugar, 2 tablespoons at a time. Fold in the flour the same way, then the flavourings. Turn into an angel cake pan that is *not* greased and bake in a 375°F oven for about 35 minutes — or until the top is brown and no imprint remains when you touch the top lightly with your finger. Invert on a funnel till cold.

CHOCOLATE ANGEL CAKE

Merely substitute ¼ **cup cocoa** for as much flour in the Angel Cake recipe.

SUNNY SPONGE CAKE

Here's how to use up the egg yolks left from the Angel Cake; it keeps well and is nice for trifle pudding later on.

> **12 egg yolks (1 cup)**
> **1½ cups sugar**
> **¾ cup warm water**
> **1 tablespoon grated orange or lemon rind (optional)**
> **½ teaspoon lemon juice or extract**
> **½ teaspoon vanilla**
> **2 cups cake flour**
> **2 teaspoons baking powder**
> **½ teaspoon salt**

Beat the egg yolks until thick, gradually add the sugar; alternately beat in the water, rind, and flavourings with the sifted flour, baking powder, and salt. Pour into an ungreased tube pan and bake at 325°F for almost an hour. Invert on a funnel till cold, then ice with a fluffy or soft icing. It's good with maple icing too.

NEVER FAIL SPONGE CAKE

This is a cake for times of celebration and for making money for good causes. Barbie and Patti often bake this one: it's big and light as an angel cake but less trouble and fewer eggs. Only one drawback — it's torn apart and eaten in a few minutes.

> **¾ teaspoon cream of tartar**
> **6 egg whites, at room temperature**
> **1½ cups sugar**
> **6 egg yolks**
> **1½ cups flour**
> **1 teaspoon baking powder**
> **½ teaspoon salt**
> **½ cup fruit juice or water**
> **1 tablespoon grated orange peel**
> **1 teaspoon vanilla or rum flavouring**

Add cream of tartar to the egg whites and beat at high speed until foamy; gradually add ¾ cup of the sugar, continuing to beat until stiff peaks form. To the egg yolks add the remaining ¾ cup sugar; sift together the flour, baking powder, and salt, add to the yolk mixture alternately with the fruit juice, orange peel, and flavouring; blend at low speed until moistened; beat 1 minute at medium speed. Pour in the egg whites and, by hand, carefully fold them in until just blended. Pur the batter into an ungreased tube pan. Bake 40 to 45 minutes in a 350°F oven. Invert and cool thoroughly before removing from the pan. Serve with fruit, whipped or ice cream. It really doesn't need any icing. Icing would weigh it down. But if you need icing for an occasion you could use Angel Feather Frosting (page 80).

POTATO FLOUR SPONGE CAKE

I followed the directions for this cake exactly, and to my surprise it came out of the oven looking like a big birthday cake. The texture was even and light as a feather. It dried out more quickly than a regular cake but after freezing made a very fine trifle pudding.

4 eggs
¾ cup sugar
½ teaspoon vanilla
¾ cup potato flour
1 teaspoon baking powder
¼ teaspoon salt
2 teaspoons lemon juice
Angel Feather Icing (page 80)

Place a mixing bowl over a pan of hot water. Add the eggs, sugar, and vanilla; beat until the mixture is lukewarm. Remove the bowl from the pan and continue beating until the mixture resembles whipped cream — it shouldn't get too stiff. Sift together the potato flour, baking powder, and salt, then sift again. Gradually fold dry ingredients into the egg mixture using a spoon or wire whisk, then fold in the lemon juice. Gently pour into an ungreased tube pan or a long shallow cake pan. Bake at 350°F for 35 to 40 minutes, or until cake springs back when lightly touched. Invert on a rack and cool in the pan for one hour. Loosen sides of cake with a spatula and remove from pan. Ice with Angel Feather Icing.

AUNT MAGDALINE'S HURRY SPONGE CAKE

You can make trifle with this cake too.

> **3 eggs**
> **1½ cups sugar**
> **2 cups flour**
> **½ cup water**
> **2 teaspoons baking powder**
> **½ teaspoon salt**
> **1 teaspoon lemon or vanilla flavouring**

Beat the eggs for 1 minute. Gradually add sugar and beat for 5 minutes. Add 1 cup of sifted flour and beat 1 minute more, then add water. Fold in remaining cup of flour sifted with baking powder and salt; stir in the flavouring. Pour into greased cake or tube pan and bake at 350°F for 25 to 30 minutes.

MILDRED'S ORANGE WALNUT CAKE

Whenever a cake is baked in a tube pan, I think it should be for a party; this is so easy to make that it needn't be. It has a super flavour and texture.

> **⅓ cup margarine or butter**
> **1 cup sugar**
> **1 teaspoon salt**
> **3 eggs, separated**
> **Rind of 1 orange, grated**
> **1 cup buttermilk**
> **2 cups flour**
> **½ teaspoon baking soda**
> **1 teaspoon baking powder**
> **1 cup finely chopped walnuts**
> **¾ cup orange juice**
> **Liqueur Butter Icing (page 76)**

Cream the margarine and sugar till light, add the salt and egg yolks, mix well. If you have a blender, put the orange peel into it with the buttermilk and whirl it till the rind is very fine; stir it into the sugar mixture. Sift the flour, baking soda, and baking powder together and blend into the batter. Fold in the walnuts, then the egg whites, stiffly beaten. Pour into a buttered tube pan. Bake in a 350°F oven for 50 minutes or slightly longer.

While you're waiting for the crucial moment, heat the orange juice — the real thing or whatever you use instead — and when the cake comes safely out of the oven, drizzle the hot juice over it with a spoon. Let the cake stay in the pan till it cools slightly then turn it out carefully on a pretty serving plate.

Make a butter icing with orange juice to moisten it, and Cointreau as the flavouring. Slather the icing on the top of the cake and let it run down the sides. It doesn't have to cover it, the cake has enough flavour without embellishment.

LAURIE BENNETT'S PUMPKIN RING

Pumpkin cakes are often rather heavy, but Laurie's was light and delicious as the Irish Mist she served with it at a dessert party on St. Patrick's Day.

   ⅓ **cup shortening**
   1⅓ **cups sugar**
   1 **egg**
   1 **cup pumpkin, cooked and mashed**
   1⅔ **cups cake flour**
   ¼ **teaspoon baking powder**
   1 **teaspoon baking soda**
   ¾ **teaspoon salt**
   ½ **teaspoon cinnamon**
   ¼ **teaspoon ground cloves**
   ⅓ **cup water**
   ⅓ **cup chopped nuts**
   ⅔ **cup raisins**
   Glaze (page 78)

Cream the shortening and sugar, beat in the egg and pumpkin. Sift together the flour, baking powder, baking soda, salt, and spices. Beat the flour mixture alternately with the water into the pumpkin mixture. Stir in by hand the chopped nuts and raisins. Pour into a greased and floured tube pan and bake in a 350°F oven for 50 minutes. Invert and cool on a rack. Laurie iced hers with a glaze that covered the inverted bottom of the cake and ran down the sides. Very neat.

LEMON-ORANGE CAKE

This slightly tart, moist, flavourful cake baked in a tube pan really has class. Try it on company and bask in their praise.

⅓ cup butter or margarine
1 cup sugar
Salt
3 eggs, separated
1 cup buttermilk
Grated rind of ½ lemon
1 whole orange rind chopped in chunks
    the size of a dime
2 cups flour
½ teaspoon baking soda
1 teaspoon baking powder

Topping:
½ cup sugar
Juice of 1 orange
Juice of ½ lemon
Orange or Lemon Butter Icing (page 76)

Cream butter and sugar. Add salt and egg yolks. Stir in the milk and rinds. Sift flour, baking soda, and baking powder into the batter and blend. Beat egg whites until stiff and fold in. Pour batter into a well-greased tube pan and bake at 375°F for 10 minutes then reduce the heat to 350°F and bake another 50 minutes or until the cake tests done. Heat all the topping ingredients, stirring until the sugar is dissolved. Pour over the hot cake. Cool in the pan about 10 minutes, invert over a rack. Ice with Orange or Lemon Butter Icing. Use just enough icing to cover the top of the cake and run down the sides.

NUTTY PEACH CAKE
(from Mrs. Omer Horst)

Baked in a tube pan, this great, moist, flavourful cake can be
cut in thin slices. But don't let that fool you: they'll all want
several pieces as on one night when fifteen people came to my
cottage and this cake and another disappeared completely.
Success!

> **2 cups flour**
> **1 teaspoon salt**
> **½ teaspoon baking powder**
> **½ teaspoon baking soda**
> **½ teaspoon cinnamon**
> **1 cup sugar**
> **¾ cup vegetable oil**
> **3 eggs**
> **1½ cups mashed peaches (unpeeled)**
> **1 teaspoon lemon juice blended with the peaches**
> **1 cup pecans or walnuts**
> **Glaze (page 78)**

Sift the dry ingredients into a bowl, add the oil, eggs, and
mashed peaches with the lemon juice over them. Beat until
they're all thoroughly combined; the batter is lovely to taste.
Stir in the nuts. Pour into a buttered and floured tube pan and
bake in a 300°F oven for about 1 hour and 15 minutes, or until
a toothpick comes out clean when you prick it.

Invert the cake on a rack and let it slide out of the pan to cool.
Drizzle glaze over top and sides.

I had trouble the first time I made this: when I turned it out
of the pan the bottom stayed in. I manoeuvred it out but the
patched result was bumpy, so I served thick slices on individual
plates with whipped cream hiding the defects and there wasn't
a crumb left — only praise for the flavour.

GERMAN BUNDT CAKE

Two little girls made this large impressive cake for the Kinderkochfest.

> 1½ cups vegetable oil
> 1½ cups sugar
> 4 eggs
> 2 teaspoons vanilla
> 1 tablespoon rum
> 1½ cups milk
> ¾ cup cocoa
> 5 cups flour
> 5 teaspoons baking powder
> ¼ teaspoon salt
>
> *Icing:*
> ¼ cup butter
> 3 tablespoons cocoa
> 1 cup icing sugar
> 3 tablespoons hot water

In a large bowl, combine oil, sugar, and eggs. Beat on high for 5 minutes. Add vanilla, rum, and milk. Mix. Sift cocoa, flour, baking powder, and salt and add to mixture. Beat again for 5 minutes. Batter will be thick. Turn into a well-greased tube or bundt pan and bake at 350°F for about 60 minutes or until toothpick inserted in centre comes out clean. When the cake has cooled, remove from the pan. Blend icing ingredients. The icing should be thin enough to pour freely from a spoon. Drizzle over cake and down the sides and centre (great for scooping up with the fingers and licking).

SPICY MARBLE CAKE

I've spent a long time looking for a good marble cake recipe. The one in *Food That Really Schmecks* is terrible: high, dry, and tasteless. Sorry about that. At last I've found one: Joan Picard, who lives in Chesley, sent me this one, moist and tasty.

½ **cup shortening**
1 **cup sugar**
2 **eggs**
2 **cups flour**
2 **teaspoons baking powder**
½ **teaspoon salt**
⅔ **cup milk**
1½ **teaspoons cinnamon**
¾ **teaspoons cloves**
¾ **teaspoon nutmeg**
¼ **cup molasses**

Cream together the shortening and sugar; add the eggs, one at a time, beating after each. Sift together the flour, baking powder, and salt; add them alternately with the milk to the creamed mixture. Divide the batter into two parts. To one part add the spices and molasses. Drop spoonfuls, alternating light and dark batters, into a greased loaf or tube pan. Draw a knife through the batter to get the marbled effect. Bake in a 350°F oven for about 50 to 60 minutes. Test it. Cool 10 minutes then remove from the pan to a rack.

CHOCOLATE MARBLE CAKE

Sometimes I want a chocolate marble cake with chocolate icing. I tried this several times before I was satisfied with it.

Follow Joan's recipe (above) to the place where you divide the batter. Then, instead of spices and molasses, to half the batter add a blend of ⅓ **cup cocoa**, ¼ **cup corn syrup**, and **1 or 2 tablespoons hot water**. The result delighted my soul. The guests I made it for each ate two thick slices and I sent them home with the cake that was left — to prevent eating it all myself.

MARIE'S MARBLE CAKE

When Marie came to my house the other day, she said she had just baked a marble cake and her husband said it was the best he'd ever tasted. She gave me her recipe.

>   5 eggs
>   2 cups sugar
>   1 teaspoon vanilla
>   2 teaspoons lemon juice
>   2 cups flour
>   2 teaspoons baking powder
>   ½ cup vegetable oil
>   2 tablespoons cocoa
>   Chocolate Icing (page 75) or
>   Angel Feather Icing (page 80)

Mix first four ingredients well together. (Marie has a mixer and she lets it run for 5 minutes.) Sift the flour and baking powder together and add it to the egg mixture then, last of all, stir or beat in the oil. Marie says that makes it light. Put ⅓ of the batter into a greased tube pan. To another third stir in some cocoa — Marie says she doesn't measure but it might be 2 tablespoons. Don't overdo it — she tells by the colour. Spoon it into the pan then spoon in the other — last —third and bake at 325°F for 50 to 60 minutes. Covered with Chocolate or Angel Feather Icing this makes an elegant birthday cake.

GUGELHUPF BIERKUCHEN
(Beer Cake)

No sugar, no eggs, an elusive flavour; this cake is a winner. It is
moist, heavy, and keeps well if you let it.

1 cup molasses
½ cup butter or margarine
1 bottle beer
1 cup raisins
2⅔ cups flour
½ teaspoon salt
1 tablespoon baking powder
¼ teaspoon baking soda
½ teaspoon cinnamon
½ teaspoon nutmeg
½ teaspoon ginger
1 cup coarsely chopped filberts or pecans

Combine the molasses, butter, and beer in a saucepan and heat
only until the butter melts; stir in the raisins and let the mixture
cool for 15 minutes. Sift together the dry ingredients. Stir in the
nuts. When the beer mixture has cooled, pour it over the dry
ingredients and stir until smooth. Pour the batter into a greased
and floured tube pan and bake in a 350°F oven for about 1 hour.
Test it. Turn it over on a cake rack and let it cool a bit before
dribbling a glaze over it.

GLAZE: Mix **1 cup icing sugar** and enough **liquid honey** to
moisten the icing sugar to the dribbly stage. Pour it over the top
of the cake and let it run down the sides. If you don't have
honey, try maple or corn syrup.

SCHWARZWAELDER KIRSCHTORTE
(Black Forest Cherry Torte)

The recipe for the winning Black Forest torte in the Kinderkochfest Competition was very long and complicated and not nearly as delicious as the version my smart niece Barbie concocted.

1 sponge cake + ⅓ cup cocoa (page 56)
½ cup Kirsch or rum or liqueur

Filling:
½ cup butter
3½ cups icing sugar
2 teaspoons very strong coffee
3 or 4 cups pitted cherries

Icing:
2 cups whipping cream
¼ cup sugar
1 teaspoon vanilla
Chocolate curls

Barbie bakes her favourite Never Fail Sponge Cake (page 56), adding ⅓ cup cocoa to be sifted with the flour. When the cake has cooled, she carefully slices it into 4 layers. She sprinkles each layer with Kirsch or rum or liqueur (½ cup all together). To make the filling, she blends together the butter, icing sugar, and coffee till creamy like icing, and spreads ⅓ of it over the bottom layer of the cake. Into it she presses ⅓ of the cherries. Barbie uses sour frozen ones. (If they have thawed, or if canned cherries are used, they should be well drained.) She repeats this operation on the next two layers, putting each layer of cake on top of the one below before she fills it. She puts the fourth layer on top. Finally she whips the cream, adds the ¼ cup sugar (less if sweet cherries are used) and the vanilla. She slathers it on top and round the sides of the cake, then decorates it with chocolate curls. The result is a triumph and should be eaten as soon as possible. No problem.

JELLY ROLL

We always hung around to watch — and to eat — when Mother made a jelly roll.

> **1 cup sugar**
> **3 eggs, beaten**
> **⅓ cup water**
> **1 teaspoon vanilla**
> **1 cup flour**
> **1 teaspoon baking powder**
> **¼ teaspoon salt**
> **Icing sugar**
> **Jelly or jam or lemon filling**

Gradually add sugar to the thickly beaten eggs, continue beating and add water and vanilla. Sift dry ingredients together and beat them in until the batter is smooth. Pour into a greased and floured 15" x 10" pan, lined with greased paper or foil. Bake at 375°F for 12 to 15 minutes — till the cake just tests done — overbaking makes it hard to remove the paper. Immediately turn the cake upside-down on a towel sprinkled with icing sugar. Quickly and carefully pull off the paper. Spread the cake at once with jelly or jam or lemon filling. Roll up, wrap in a towel until cool and don't keep it too long before you serve it.

CHRISTMAS AND FRUIT CAKES

MOTHER'S DARK FRUIT CAKE

This very morning I found this recipe written in Mother's fine legible script, and it made me remember how lovingly and carefully she made this cake every Christmas and for each of our weddings. It always turned out well and I think she was proud of it.

> 1⅓ cups brown sugar
> 1 cup butter, melted
> 4 eggs, well beaten
> ½ cup wine or whisky
> ½ cup medium molasses
> 2 cups flour
> 1 teaspoon baking soda
> ½ teaspoon baking powder
> 1 teaspoon cinnamon
> ¾ teaspoon cloves
> Pinch of nutmeg
> 1 cup sliced or chopped citron and lemon peel
> 2 cups raisins
> 1 cup chopped dates
> 1 cup chopped almonds or Brazil nuts
> ½ cup candied cherries

Line 2 loaf pans or 1 large round pan with heavy wax paper, buttered. Cream sugar and butter. Add eggs, whisky, and molasses. Sift together flour, baking soda, baking powder, and spices. Stir in peel, raisins, dates, nuts, and cherries. Pour in a cake pan and bake in a 350°F oven. Mother has written, "It says bake 3 hours but I don't think it takes 3 hours. After an hour keep trying it." Mother says the cake burns easily on the bottom so she puts 2 cookie sheets in the bottom of the oven to divert the heat. After the cake had cooled, Mother used to drizzle some wine or whisky over it to keep it moist for a long time.

LIGHT CHRISTMAS FRUIT CAKE

My favourite; it has a mild, fruity flavour.

> **1 cup butter**
> **½ cup sugar**
> **3 eggs**
> **2 teaspoons vanilla**
> **1 teaspoon almond flavouring**
> **1 teaspoon lemon flavouring (or juice)**
> **2¾ cups flour**
> **1 teaspoon baking powder**
> **1 teaspoon nutmeg**
> **½ teaspoon salt**
> **2¾ cups raisins**
> **1½ cups candied red cherries, cut up**
> **1 cup canned pineapple, cut up**
> **¾ cup candied green cherries, cut up**
> **1 cup mixed peel, cut or sliced thin**
> **1 cup almonds, sliced lengthwise**
> **1 cup additional almonds for topping**

Blend butter and sugar; add eggs, one at a time, and beat; add flavourings, sifted dry ingredients, fruit, peel, and nuts; mix well. Grease sheet of brown paper with shortening, fit carefully into a large loaf pan — or two smaller ones. Turn cake into pan, cover with cup of sliced almonds, pressed slightly into the dough to make them stick. Bake at 250° to 350°F for 3 hours.

CHRISTMAS CAKE AT RUNDLES

John Walker, the *chef de cuisine* at Rundles restaurant in Stratford, Ontario, made this a month before Christmas. He covered it with his own almond paste, let it rest for a couple of weeks before icing it glamorously with scrolls and rosettes, applied with a pastry tube. As he wrote "Merry Christmas" on the top, he said, "Never abbreviate the word 'Christmas', it's vulgar."

> 2¼ cups raisins (large ones)
> 2¼ cups currants
> 2¼ cups sultanas (small raisins)
> ¾ cup cherries
> ½ cup whole almonds
> ½ cup ground almonds
> ¾ cup chopped peel
> Grated rind of 1 lemon and 1 orange
> 1 glass whisky
> 1 cup butter or margarine
> 1 cup brown sugar, packed
> 6 eggs, beaten
> 2½ cups flour
> 1 teaspoon cinnamon or cloves

Line a large round or square tin with greaseproof paper. Clean the fruit; cut the cherries into halves or quarters. Blanch the whole almonds and chop them. Mix the fruit, nuts, ground almonds, peel, and grated rind. Add ⅛ of the whisky and leave for about 1 hour. (The size of the glass of whisky was never disclosed, but Leslie, the *sous-chef*, said, "We put in lots of booze.") Beat the butter and sugar, add the beaten eggs, mix the sifted flour and spice. Fold in the fruit. Spoon into the prepared tin. Put into the oven at 325°F for 1 hour, then reduce to 300°F and bake about 2 hours more. Pour remainder of whisky over the cake and leave to cool. When cold, remove from the tin and wrap in foil until Christmas, unless you want to put on almond paste and icing.

HAROLD HORWOOD'S GREAT AUNT LILLIAN'S FIG CAKE

Fig cakes are a long-standing tradition in Newfoundland where salt fish has been traded to the Mediterranean for hundreds of years, many of the vessels that sailed outward with fish returning with barrels of dried figs among other things. Great Aunt Lillian got this cake from her grandmother but she has improved it a little by substituting modern ingredients not available in her grandmother's time. She says that such things as wheat germ and corn oil make cakes taste better as well as making them more nutritious. Harold goes on: "I made Aunt Lillian's fig cake for Christmas and it turned out so well that I've made it again since. It is such an easy cake and so good and popular with visitors that I thought I ought to send you the recipe. The proportions of fruit are hardly critical. The cake is very soft and moist. The figs give it a special flavour and texture that I personally find very pleasant."

4 cups (1½ pounds) chopped figs
2½ cups (1 pound) dates, chopped
   (Aunt Lillian sometimes uses raisins instead)
1 cup hot water
2 eggs
½ cup corn (or sunflower)oil
½ cup molasses
½ cup brown sugar
1 teaspoon allspice
1 teaspoon cinnamon
2½ cups flour
1 cup wheat germ
1 teaspoon baking soda, dissolved in ½ cup
   hot water

Steep figs and dates in hot water. Leave until soft. Beat eggs, oil, molasses, sugar, and spices. Add to softened fruit. Stir in remaining ingredients. Aunt Lillian bakes it in a paper-lined iron pot at 300°F for 1 hour and 20 minutes. I bake it in an oiled steel bowl for the same time. In a cake ring, it should be ready in about an hour.

JEAN SALTER'S BOILED FRUIT CAKE

Jeannie got this recipe from her auntie in England who made a specialty of it because everyone liked it so well.

> **2 cups mixed dried fruit**
> **1 cup butter**
> **1¼ cups water**
> **1 cup sugar**
> **½ teaspoon vanilla**
> **1 teaspoon baking soda**
> **1 egg, beaten**
> **2 cups flour**
> **Spices according to taste:**
> **cinnamon, ginger, nutmeg, etc.**
> **1½ teaspoons baking powder**

Combine the first four ingredients in a large saucepan and bring to the boil. Remove from the stove and stir in the vanilla and baking soda. Leave to cool, then add the beaten egg, then the combined flour and spices and baking powder. Mix well, put in a buttered cake tin and bake in a 325°F oven for about 1¼ hours.

PINEAPPLE COCONUT FRUITCAKE
3 small loaves

Marg Phelan had this recipe photocopied because so many people who ate it at her house wanted to make it.

> **1½ cups diced candied pineapple**
> **1½ cups light raisins**
> **½ cup diced orange peel**
> **1 cup chopped walnuts**
> **2 cups flaked coconut**
> **1 cup butter**

1 cup sugar (Marg says she uses less)
4 eggs
1 cup pineapple juice
2 cups flour
1 teaspoon baking powder
1 teaspoon salt

Combine the fruits, nuts, and coconut. Cream the butter and sugar until fluffy. Add the eggs, beating well after each one. Stir in the pineapple juice. Sift together the flour, baking powder, and salt; add to the sugar mixture. Fold in the fruit. Spoon into three 8" x 4" buttered and floured loaf pans. Bake in a 300°F oven for 1½ hours, but look before that. Cool, remove from the pans. Wrap separately and store in a cool place for 2 weeks before you cut it. No cheating.

JEAN SALTER'S RICH SEED CAKE
6-inch loaf pan

Jean got this recipe from her English grandmother. Because it was simple and easy she baked it in the trim little galley of the vessel that she and her husband Don sailed from England to Barbados. It has a fine, firm texture the colour of daffodils.

2 cups flour
½ teaspoon salt
½ teaspoon baking powder
2 teaspoons caraway seeds
¾ cup butter or margarine
¾ cup sugar
2 or 3 eggs
A little milk

Sift the dry ingredients and add the seeds. Cream the butter and sugar and beat in the eggs gradually. Add the dry ingredients and, if necessary, enough milk to give a dropping consistency. If you like, you could add a teaspoon of vanilla or a tablespoon of brandy. Put the rather thick batter in a 6-inch loaf pan and bake at 350°F for about an hour. Cut it in thin slices and serve it with tea. It doesn't need icing.

ANGIE'S RAVISHING RAISIN CAKE
2 loaves

This is a "keeper."

> 2½ cups seedless raisins
> 2¼ cups boiling water
> ⅔ cup shortening
> ¾ cup white sugar
> ¾ cup brown sugar
> 3 cups flour
> 1½ teaspoons salt
> 1½ teaspoons baking soda
> ¼ teaspoon nutmeg
> ½ teaspoon cloves
> 1 teaspoon cinnamon
> 1 cup coarsely chopped nuts
> 1 cup buttermilk
> 2 teaspoons vanilla

Boil the raisins in the water until there is almost no water left — no more than a couple of tablespoonfuls. Add the shortening and stir until it is melted, then the sugars and stir until they are completely dissolved. Add the sifted dry ingredients and nuts alternately with the milk and vanilla, beating well after each addition. Pour into two greased loaf pans and bake at 325°F for an hour or until cake tests done.

FROSTINGS AND FILLINGS

BASIC BUTTER ICING

You can't make a mistake with a plain butter icing; plenty of beating makes it quite fluffy. There are also as many variations as you care to invent. When Norm makes cookies that call for butter or margarine, she always uses butter, but for icings she uses margarine because the icing becomes fluffier and stays moister.

> **4 tablespoons soft butter or margarine**
> **1½ cups icing sugar**
> **Pinch of salt**
> **1 to 2 tablespoons milk, cream, water, fruit juice, or coffee**
> **1 teaspoon vanilla, rum, or any flavouring**

Cream the butter or margarine and gradually work in half the sugar. Add salt, liquid, and flavouring, then work in the remaining sugar (or enough to make the icing spread easily). You can't miss: you just keep adding sugar or liquid until the spreadability is perfect. For layer cakes, just double or triple the amounts. If you want it richer, add more butter.

CHOCOLATE BUTTER ICING

Add ⅓ cup cocoa or 2 ounces of melted unsweetened chocolate to Basic Butter Icing.

COFFEE BUTTER ICING

Use strong coffee for the liquid or add a teaspoon or a tablespoon of instant coffee powder to the basic recipe. I like a combination of chocolate and coffee myself.

ALMOND BUTTER ICING

Almond flavouring added to Basic Butter Icing is all you need, but you might like to add toasted almonds as well — or sprinkle them on top.

Orange or Lemon Butter Icing

Use orange juice or lemon juice as your liquid and flavouring, plus a teaspoon of grated rind.

Liqueur Butter Icing

Any liqueurs, rum, crème de cacao, crème de menthe, Cointreau, whisky, Tia Maria, or whatever you have; a pleasant surprise and taste — as a flavouring, or even as the liquid in your icing.

Coloured Butter Icing

Simply add a very little bit of fruit colouring to basic icing to get the colour you want. But be careful — shocking pink or indigo is not appetizing.

SOFT MAPLE ICING

¼ cup soft butter
½ cup maple syrup
½ teaspoon vanilla
2½ cups icing sugar

Blend butter, syrup, and vanilla till smooth, then add gradually and blend in the icing sugar. Delicious, easy to spread — and it stays soft.

PEANUT BUTTER ICING

Blend **¼ cup butter or margarine** with **⅓ cup peanut butter** and **⅓ teaspoon salt**. Add **2¼ cups sifted icing sugar** and **½ cup strong cold coffee**, alternately, a little at a time. Cream after each addition till smooth.

Baked-on Frostings

These are so simple to do and so good when toasted under the broiler. They give something special to many kinds of cake — plain white, spice, banana, oatmeal, even chocolate. Let your cake cool for about 5 minutes, spread the icing over the top, quickly, then put it under your broiler until it bubbles and becomes lightly browned — keep watching it all the time, it doesn't take long.

TOASTED COCONUT FROSTING

⅓ cup brown sugar
2 tablespoons cream
¾ cup shredded coconut
½ cup walnuts or pecans or almonds (optional)

Combine ingredients. Spread on cake, then put under broiler until frosting bubbles.

BAKED-ON BUTTERSCOTCH FROSTING

3 tablespoons butter, melted
¾ cup brown sugar
4 tablespoons cream
½ cup coconut or chopped nuts

Mix, spread on cake while it is warm and put under the broiler until it begins to bubble.

LAZY BAKED-ON ICING

Sometimes when I'm in a hurry I simply sprinkle a fairly thick cake batter with a mixture of sugar and nuts — not too thick or it will sink. Or I make crumbs — with **1 cup brown sugar**, **3 tablespoons butter** and **3 tablespoons flour** — and spread them over the batter, or baked cake, and bake them or brown them.

BAKED-ON MERINGUE ICING

2 egg whites
Pinch of salt
¼ teaspoon cream of tartar
1 cup brown sugar
1 cup chopped nuts or coconut — or both

Beat egg whites till stiff, adding salt and cream of tartar; a bit at a time, add the brown sugar, beating until smooth. Spread over cake and sprinkle with nuts or coconut — bake at 350°F until bubbly.

BAKED-ON MARSHMALLOW ICING

12 marshmallows
½ cup brown sugar
½ cup chopped nuts

Cut the marshmallows in half, crosswise, place them on the unbaked, thick batter of your cake — (or on the baked cake that has cooled for 5 minutes) — mix the sugar and nuts and sprinkle over the marshmallows and bake on the cake or broil until slightly bubbly.

GLAZE

An ideal icing for buns, coffee cakes, or tube cakes that need a thin icing on top that will run down the sides.

1¼ cups icing sugar
1¼ tablespoons butter, softened
1 teaspoon vanilla or other flavouring
1½ tablespoons boiling water

Sift the sugar into a bowl; blend in the butter, vanilla, and boiling water, beating until it is smooth, adding more boiling water drop by drop if necessary. Beat several minutes until it is creamy then spread it on lukewarm buns, cake, etc.

MARSHMALLOW CHOCOLATE CHIP ICING

This would make any cake look good and taste even better.

1½ cups miniature marshmallows,
**   or large ones cut up**
1 cup chocolate chips
4 tablespoons milk or cream

Put everything into the top of a double boiler and heat over boiling water, stirring until the chocolate and marshmallows are melted. Spread quickly over the cake.

LORNA'S SUPER CHOCOLATE CHIP ICING
for 2 layers

This has that real chocolate flavour and it stays soft.

6 ounces semi-sweet chocolate pieces
½ cup light cream
1 cup margarine or butter
2½ cups icing sugar

In a saucepan combine the chocolate, cream, and margarine; stir till smooth, remove from heat and whisk in the icing sugar — it will be thin. Beat it over ice till it holds shape (put ice cubes and water in a bowl with the saucepan on top).

Of course, I hadn't time to do that so I used only ¼ cup cream and after I'd whisked in the icing sugar I set the saucepan in my fridge till the icing had set and then iced the cake. If you hadn't eaten Lorna's icing and known it was better, you'd have thought mine was pretty good, too.

FLUFFY MAPLE ICING

Boil **1½ cups maple syrup** until it spins a long thread; pour it slowly over the **stiffly beaten whites of 2 eggs**, whipping steadily during the process.

RAISIN ORANGE ICING
for 2 layers

Smooth, moist, tart, and especially good on cakes that have spices or fruit

½ **cup raisins**
Rind of ½ orange
Juice of 1 orange (⅓ cup)
2 tablespoons butter
2 tablespoons cream or whole milk
2½ to 3 cups icing sugar

Put everything but the sugar into your blender and blend until the raisins are fine. Gradually add the sugar, while blending, until you have added 1 cupful. Scrape it into a bowl and keep adding enough sugar to make smooth, spreadable icing.

ANGEL FEATHER ICING

There's nothing better for an angel cake or a layer cake than this almost foolproof and luscious icing; it doesn't dissolve, run away or get crusty; it stays tender and fluffy for days if anyone lets it last that long.

2 egg whites
¾ **cup sugar**
⅓ **cup corn syrup**
2 tablespoons water
¼ **teaspoon cream of tartar**
¼ **teaspoon salt**
1 teaspoon vanilla or other flavouring

Put everything but the vanilla into the top of a double boiler with fast-boiling water below. Start beating immediately with a rotary beater or electric mixer until the mixture stands in stiff peaks. Remove from heat, add flavouring, and keep on beating until it is thick enough to spread easily. You'll be delighted and everyone will exclaim when they see the glorified cake.

COCOA FUDGE ICING.

Really fudgy, easy to make and almost foolproof.

1 cup sugar, brown or white
¼ cup cocoa
¼ cup milk
¼ cup butter
½ teaspoon vanilla

In a saucepan, combine the sugar and cocoa, stir in the milk till it's smooth, drop in the butter and stir over moderate heat. Boil for *one* minute only. Remove from heat and cool as quickly as you can (put pan in cold water in the sink). Stir in the vanilla and beat until it's creamy and thick. It stays soft — but firm — on the cake.

BOILED CHOCOLATE ICING

1 cup sugar
2 tablespoons cocoa — more if you like it really dark
Pinch of salt
3 tablespoons cornstarch
1 cup boiling water
1 tablespoon butter
1 teaspoon vanilla

In a saucepan, combine sugar, cocoa, salt, and cornstarch. Stir in water, bring to a boil, and cook, stirring, until thick. Remove from heat and stir in butter and vanilla. Let cool, then spread on cake.

PEACH DESSERT ICING

Slather a plain light layer cake with whipped cream, between the layers and on top and sides, putting peach-halves between the layers, round the rim on top (either fresh or canned peaches will do).

SOFT CHOCOLATE ICING
for 2 layers

Richly chocolate in flavour, this foolproof icing stays soft, moist, glossy, and keeps the cake that way too.

> **2 squares unsweetened chocolate, cut in pieces —**
> **or ½ cup cocoa**
> **1¼ cups milk (or strong coffee)**
> **4 tablespoons flour**
> **1 cup sugar**
> **2 tablespoons butter**
> **1 teaspoon vanilla**

Add the chocolate to the milk in a double boiler and heat. When the chocolate is melted, mix with a beater until blended. Sift flour with sugar, add a small amount of chocolate mixture, stirring until smooth; return to double boiler, cook until thickened, add butter and vanilla. Cool and spread on cake.

If you make it with cocoa, mix the sugar, flour, and cocoa in a bowl while you heat the milk in the double boiler, then pour enough of the milk into the dry mixture to make it pour nicely into the scalded milk and carry on as I've told you above.

MOCHA OR CHOCOLATE MOCHA FROSTING

> **½ cup margarine or butter**
> **¾ cup icing sugar**
> **Pinch of salt**
> **1 teaspoon vanilla or rum**
> **1 egg yolk**
> **2 tablespoons cocoa**
> **3 tablespoons very strong coffee**

Cream the margarine, sugar, and salt. Beat in the vanilla and egg yolk, then blend in the cocoa and enough coffee to make a good spreading consistency.

EVA'S WHIPPED ICING
to fill and ice a large torte

Eva says it whips up real nice and can be stored in the fridge for future use. It's smooth, delicious, and makes a cake look like a dream.

2 tablespoons cornstarch
½ cup milk
½ cup double-strength coffee
1 cup sugar
1 cup butter at room temperature,
don't use a substitute
1 teaspoon vanilla or preferred flavouring

Stir together until smooth the cornstarch and milk, then stir in the hot coffee and cook over moderate heat, stirring until thick. Remove from the heat and cool. Into a beater bowl measure the sugar, butter, vanilla, and beat until snowy white, about 10 minutes, scraping down the sides of the bowl several times. Add the cool cornstarch mixture and beat at high speed for 10 to 15 minutes more, or until it is like whipped cream. Eva says you can get almost the same effect by using 1 cup of milk — omitting the coffee — and only ½ cup butter.

MAPLE WALNUT ICING

½ cup butter
1 cup brown sugar
¼ cup milk
1¾ cups icing sugar, more or less
1 teaspoon maple flavouring
½ cup broken nuts

Melt the butter in a saucepan over moderate heat until lightly browned. Stir in the brown sugar and keep stirring until the mixture is bubbling (it will separate). Remove from the heat and stir in the milk. Return to moderate heat and bring back to just boiling, stirring constantly. Off the heat stir in icing sugar gradually. Add a little cream if necessary to make right consistency to spread. Stir in the maple flavouring and nuts.

CARAMEL ICING

This can be made quickly and is guaranteed to make any cake that needs enhancing into one that will make you eat two or three pieces.

   ¼cup butter
   1 cup brown sugar
   ⅓cup sweet or sour cream or milk

Put everything into a saucepan and bring to a boil. Boil for 2 minutes only. Cool, then beat for a few minutes. Pour on the cake, then spread. This is good on anything that has spices or a mild flavour that wants to be dominated by the maple cream flavour.

PENUCHE ICING

Soft, creamy, and delicious, my favourite on many cakes: spice, oatmeal, banana especially. Can be easily expanded to cover several layers — or eaten as candy.

   2⅔cups brown sugar
   ⅔cup milk
   ⅔cup butter
   ½teaspoon salt

Stir over low heat, then bring rapidly to full boil, stirring constantly. Boil to 220°F, or exactly 1 minute. Remove from heat, beat until lukewarm, no longer glossy, and of the right consistency to spread. If, by some fluke of fate, it doesn't get thick enough, you can (1) boil it again, adding 2 tablespoons of cornstarch or flour to thicken it or (2) enjoy scraping it off the plate as it runs down the sides of the cake.

BUTTERSCOTCH ICING

Mix **1 cup brown sugar, 1 tablespoon butter, 3 tablespoons milk** in a saucepan and let come to a boil, no more. Take from stove and add enough **icing sugar** to make a mixture that is just right for spreading over your cake. Flavour with **vanilla or rum**. It will not harden.

MOISTENERS

If you have a cake that is going a bit stale, or if you want to keep a cake moist, you might try the following:

Dissolve ½ cup sugar in **1 cup orange juice** or in ¾ cup lemon juice and ½ cup water; dribble the mixture over a stale cake — or as soon as you take a cake out of the oven.

Some people use the same trick with rum and water; others use wine.

RAISIN FILLING

Delicious between the layers of almost any cake, but especially with spice or oatmeal cakes.

¾ cup sugar
1 tablespoon cornstarch
1 cup water
1 cup raisins
3 tablespoons butter

Blend sugar and cornstarch, then the water. Add raisins and cook the mixture in a heavy saucepan or a double boiler until it is thick and clear. Remove from the heat, add butter and stir into mixture until it disappears. Spread between layers and on top of cake, too, if you like. It will keep it moist and give it a "wonderful-good" flavour.

DATE FILLING

1 cup chopped dates
½ cup sugar
1 tablespoon flour
½ cup water

Cook slowly together until thickened, stirring constantly. When almost cold, spread over the bottom layer of a cake. Some date addicts have been known to double the recipe and put a layer under the icing of a chocolate cake. Not me.

ORANGE FILLING

Good between layers of an orange, raisin, spice, graham wafer, or white cake.

    3 tablespoons sugar
    1 tablespoon cornstarch
    1 egg yolk
    Juice of 1 orange
    1 tablespoon lemon juice
    Grated rind of ½ orange
    ½ cup hot water
    1 tablespoon butter

Mix the sugar and cornstarch, add the egg yolk, then the fruit juices, orange rind, and hot water. Cook in double boiler until of consistency to spread. Stir in the butter till blended.

LEMON FILLING

Enough to fill one jelly roll or two layers of a cake.

    ¾ cup sugar
    3 tablespoons cornstarch or clearjel
    Pinch of salt
    ¾ cup water
    2 egg yolks, slightly beaten
    Juice of 1 lemon
    Grated zest of half lemon
    1 tablespoon butter

Combine sugar, cornstarch, salt, and water. Stirring constantly, cook over medium heat until mixture boils for one minute. Blend a small amount of hot mixture into egg yolks then return to saucepan, mixing in well. Gradually stir in the lemon juice, zest and butter; cook just until the mixture is of consistency to spread. Cool before spreading.

CREAM FILLING

With bananas sliced over it, this will transform a light layer cake into a Banana Cream Pie.

**2 cups milk
1 cup sugar
¹⁄₃cup flour
¹⁄₄teaspoon salt
2 eggs, slightly beaten
2 tablespoons butter
1 teaspoon vanilla or rum or almond flavouring**

Scald the milk. Mix the sugar, flour, and salt and blend in the scalded milk. Stir and cook over low heat or in a double boiler until thickened. Quickly blend in the beaten eggs and stir over heat for 2 minutes more. Add butter and flavouring. Cool and spread.

ICING TO KEEP A FRUIT CAKE MOIST

Mrs. Moore, who came from the U.S. to live in Bamburg with her grandson, sent me this recipe. She wrote: "I sent this in to a St. Petersburg, Florida, paper and got $5.00 for it."

**1 large sweet potato, baked
1 teaspoon butter
1 teaspoon vanilla
Icing sugar**

Scoop out the baked sweet potato from the skin, mix with the butter and vanilla and work in enough powdered sugar to make it right for spreading.

INDEX

FROSTINGS AND FILLINGS